Practical Incubation

Practical Incubation

Rob L. Harvey

*First published 1990
by Rob Harvey, Birdworld
Holt Pound, Nr. Farnham, Surrey GU10 4LD*

©*1990 Rob Harvey*
ISBN 0 9516540 0 x

*Printed in Great Britain by
Channel Print
Bournemouth*

All rights reserved. No part of this book may be reprinted, or reproduced or utilized in any form or by any electronic, mechanical or other means, now known or hereafter invented, including photocopying and recording, or in any information storage and retrieval system, without permission in writing from the publisher.

Forward

Having known Rob Harvey's parents, and their superb "Birdworld" for many years, I can almost, but not quite, claim to have watched Rob grow up out of short trousers.

I have, however, over the years, watched him develop his managerial skills with the birds, and watched and encouraged his interest in incubation, to see it ultimately become an obsession worse than my own.

The constantly improving care and management of the birds in "Birdworld" meant that there was an ever increasing number of breeding pairs of birds, and an ever increasing number of eggs, whose only chance of survival lay in artificial incubation

Rob very rapidly grasped the fundamentals of incubation and has set up a superb unit in which to do it, and to rear the resulting chicks.

He has also developed skills and techniques, particularly with hygiene and the monitoring and control of humidity in response to egg density calculations, that ensure that an ever increasing stream of eggs entering his incubation unit, emerge at the other end as birds.

His meticulous attention to the detail of the progress of individual eggs has begun to show the species variation in their requirement for different turning techniques.

Parrots, penguins, pigeons, owls, hawks and woodpeckers as well as all the rest; he has developed a standard tecnique for all of them. This is a book of practical procedures, in which he shares he shares his knowledge. I wish both Rob and his book every success.

Dr. ARTHUR ANDERSON BROWN
AUTHOR OF "THE INCUBATION BOOK"

Dedication

I would like to dedicate this book to my parents and a close friend. With my parents support have been able to expand my interest in incubation. In 1988 they allowed me to build my Incubation Research Station and I thank them for that.

Doug Taylor has been a close friend of my parents for over twenty years. Ever since I can remember he has been giving me advice on how to keep birds and it has always been most welcome. He is the sort of person that would help anyone at anytime and has helped me countless times, thank you Doug.

Contents

Foreword	page v
Dedication	page vi
Preface	page ix
Acknowledgements	xi

SECTION ONE:

1. **Before You Start**

1.A Beware
1.B Do I incubate or not?
1.C Which is the best method of incubation for you?
1.D Nest site hygiene
1.E Egg collecting
1.F Handling an egg
1.G The incubation room
1.H Setting up and testing your incubator
1.I Records

SECTION TWO:

2. **Basic Incubation**

2.A Hygiene
2.B Cleaning eggs
2.C Thermometers
2.D Wet bulb thermometers
2.E Moving-air incubators
2.F Still-air incubators
2.G Turning eggs

SECTION THREE:

3. Monitoring Your Eggs
3.A   Candling
3.B   Weight loss techniques
3.C   Density loss techniques

SECTION FOUR:

4. Other Considerations
4.A   Storing eggs
4.B   Bantams as incubators
4.C   Using broodies and incubators together
4.D   Hatching time
4.E   Detective work on failures
4.F   Computers and monitoring equipment

SECTION FIVE:

5.
Reference Section
5.A   Incubation periods
5.B   Manufacturers of incubators
5.C   Conversion charts
5.D   Pictures of development
5.E   References

Preface

Artificial incubation of bird eggs can be very confusing for the beginner. There are many "old wives' tales" about how this or that should be done and it seems that if you need some advice on a particular point, every person you speak to gives a slightly different answer. Over the past few years during the winter months I have given incubation courses at Birdworld. During these courses, I made a note of the main questions that were asked and collected them together. Often it was the basic ideas and procedures which produced the main confusion.

Using this information, together with my experience of incubation from the Incubation Research Station at Birdworld, I sat down and wrote this book. My aim was provide an easy to read text on incubation for the beginner. I hope that I have covered all of the import aspects of artificial incubation using easy to understand terms. I look forward to some feedback from the readers of this book. I welcome any correspondance from anyone who wishes to ask me specific questions or raise particular points. All these comments will improve my understanding of incubation and will hopefully contribute to the second expanded edition of Practical Incubation.

Rob Harvey

Acknowledgements

I would like to thank several people who have helped with my work on incubation. Firstly Dr A. Anderson Brown who was a great friend and had a vast knowledge on incubation. Every time I had a new idea or a new problem he would always be ready to talk about it on the other end of the phone.
Secondly Gary Robbins, manufacturer of A.B. Incubators,He has been extremely helpful to me over the past few years. I often need a new piece of equipment for an incubator or need to modify an incubator. On every occasion he has come up with something which I will test to the limit. He once said to me "if I can keep you happy then I can keep any customer happy". I think it was a compliment? Also I would like to thank Gary for all the help and advice he has given me on how to write and publish this book.
Many thanks to Judith Nicolas at Databird Worldwide, who is an expert at incubating parrot eggs and rearing the young. I first heard about egg density from Judith and she had no hesitation at all in showing me exactly how egg density can be used. Since that day I have used egg density techniques on eggs from tanagers to ostriches and spent many hours discussing the results with Judith. I would also like to mention that Judith has started many research projects connected with aviculture that will help us all in years to come.
I would like to thank Mrs B. Tolhurst for letting me use her excellent photos of the development of the chick embryo in relation to the shell, yolk. albumen and extra-embryonic membranes.
I would also like to thank Michael J. Webberely for the superb photography.

1 Before You Start

1.A Beware

It often seems to happen that one person can hatch eggs of a particular species but when other people try they seem to have great problems, even when the same incubator is used. There can be many reasons for this and here are a few examples to try and help you understand what happens.

Example 1.

Mr A successfully incubates and hatches the eggs of one particular species of birds. The temperature he uses according to his thermometer is 102°F. He recommends this temperature to Mr B who is grateful for the information and sets up his incubator at the same temperature.

All Mr B's eggs die !

The reason could be very simple indeed. Mr A's thermometer is reading two degrees higher, so he is actually incubating his eggs at 100°F not 102°F. Mr B's eggs were all too hot and therefore died.

Example 2.

Mr C and Mr D have eggs from the same species, use the same equipment and incubate at the same temperature. Mr C hatches his eggs successfully but Mr D only manages to hatch a few of his. Neither Mr C nor Mr D add water to their incubators.

PRACTICAL INCUBATION

The reason Mr C is much more successful than Mr D could be simply due to where they live. Mr C lives very close to a river or lake and the air is very moist, so he does not need to add any water to his incubator. Mr D lives in a very dry area, to hatch his eggs successfully he would need to add water to his incubators during incubation.

Example 3.

Mr E and Mr F use the same incubators, same temperature, same humidity and same turning. Mr E hatches eggs very successfully. Mr F seems to have great problems!

Mr E forgot to mention to Mr F that he lets his birds sit on their eggs for two weeks before he takes them.

The temperature, humidity or turning Mr E is using could be wrong but the most critical period of incubation for an egg is the first 65% of the incubation period. After this time the egg can cope with slight variations in temperature, humidity or turning without adverse effect. Mr F is incubating from day one so he is using the wrong incubation conditions to hatch his eggs.

These examples are typical of what happens when information is passed on to other people. So when you are seeking some advice, make sure you ask exactly how they are incubating their eggs, or better still, go and see for yourself.

Another problem often arises when eggs are hatched in a still-air incubator and the temperature they were successfully hatched at is then used in a moving air incubator.

Often the thermometer in a still-air incubator does not give a true reading. Still-air incubators have a large temperature gradient of several degrees from top to bottom. If the temperature is used in a moving-air incubator all the eggs would die!

As more research is being done on incubation, we find different techniques are needed for different species. Do not presume that all pheasant, all duck or all parrot eggs will need the same incubation conditions.

When something goes wrong it never seems to be human error but is always due to bad or faulty equipment. The truth is that success or failure is 90% due to the operator and 10% due to the equipment used.

BEFORE YOU START

1.B Do I Incubate The Egg Or Not?

This can be an agonising decision to make.

With parrots, a good policy to follow is to take the first two clutches of eggs as they are laid and leave the third clutch.

Most parrots will lay three clutches of eggs if the first two are taken. This way you obtain maximum results from each pair of your parrots but still allow your birds to incubate and rear one clutch of eggs. I would suggest not to be too greedy and try for a fourth as the female will be a bit worn out after laying so many eggs.

Maximum results are not just important for financial reasons. Many species of parrots are now in danger of becoming extinct, and many more will soon join the list, so the chance to produce three times the amount of young from each pair of parrots is highly relevant.

I prefer parent-reared chicks for breeding stock but this is a preference rather than a necessity.

With most species of pheasant, it is not a good idea to let the adult birds sit on their own eggs as they do not seem to be very good at it. On the other hand I do like to give each pair of pheasants at least one chance of incubating their own eggs and possibly rearing their young, because if a pair of pheasants are successful, then they will normally be successful every year.

If you want to find out whether or not your pheasants are capable of incubating their eggs and rearing the young, I would suggest you pull the first clutch of eggs and when the second clutch is laid, pull the eggs but replace them with fertile bantam eggs. This way you do not waste any of your precious eggs and you will find out if your adult birds will make good parents or not.

If you are dealing with a pair of birds, the young of which you do not know how to hand rear, then it is probably best to leave the eggs. However if they have already lost several clutches then you do not have anything to lose by incubating the eggs and trying to rear the youngsters.

Every pair of birds can need slightly different treatment. For example, I have a pair of Bleeding Heart Doves which lay fertile eggs but never sit on them properly. The developing embryos have always died at a few days old. Eggs taken as laid are easy to incubate but rearing the young by hand has proved to be almost impossible.

PRACTICAL INCUBATION

Eventually I found the answer. The eggs are taken as they are laid and replaced with dummy eggs. The fertile eggs are artificially incubated, and as soon as they externally pip, they are swapped over with the dummy eggs. The adult birds are good at rearing the young chicks.

This method has been used several times with these birds with great success. So it seems that if a particular pair of birds do not sit well, it will not always follow that they cannot rear their young.

1.C Which is the best method of incubation for you?

You can spend a fortune on incubation equipment but that does not mean you will achieve good results. Consider how much time you are willing to spend and then how much money! The best way to illustrate this is by examples:

A.

If you are going to keep a few ducks or pheasants and wish to artificially incubate the eggs, the simplest and cheapest method would be to use broody bantams (See page 72).

If you want to try an incubator, before you buy one, try and get as much advice as possible from people who are successfully hatching eggs at the moment. If you can go on an incubation course, so much the better.

A small piece of advice, because you are entering a mine-field. You will get slightly different advice from every person you talk to, so I suggest you listen to everyone and then make up your own mind!! If time is a problem for you, then an incubator with automatic turning would be essential.

B

If you keep parrots or exotic birds, using bantams as incubators is not realistic.

The first question then becomes do I use a still-air incubator or a moving-air-incubator. Information on both types is on pages 24 and 33.

BEFORE YOU START

Personally I would suggest using a moving-air incubator for beginners because the temperature is fairly constant throughout the incubator. In still-air machines there is temperature gradient from top to bottom which can be very confusing.

Good results mainly come from experience and knowing your incubator. Some people swear by still-air machines and say that moving-air incubators are useless. This is because they are used to still-air machines and get good results so they do not want to change. If you are getting good results using whatever incubator, don't change!!

How far should you go?

This depends on how much money you can afford to spend. A good moving air incubator with automatic turning is not cheap, and with automatic humidity the price goes up again.

The next step would be applying weight-loss techniques, but an accurate set of scales involves more money. Then perhaps two incubators, a hatcher, a good candler .... I could keep going!

Once you go out and meet people who are using incubators you will get a better idea of what you will need for your own set-up.

So the best thing for the beginner to do is to go on an incubation course, pester a few people who are successfully hatching eggs, read up about the eggs you want to incubate and then buy an incubator.

REMEMBER GOOD RESULTS OR FAILURES ARE NORMALLY 90% DUE TO HUMANS AND 10% DUE TO INCUBATORS!

1.D Nest Site Hygiene

This is something which many people seem to neglect. You can clean and sterilise your eggs as much as you like, but if the nest site is dirty there will be millions of bacteria waiting to attack the egg as it is laid.

As soon as the egg is laid, it cools and therefore sucks in air through the pores in the shell and if large numbers of bacteria are there as well, it will suck them in too. So by the time you pick up your egg it could already be too late to save it.

PRACTICAL INCUBATION

If bacteria have already penetrated the egg shell and membranes they may not kill the developing embryo immediately; in fact the embryo could develop and the egg hatch, but the chick can die within a week of hatching with a yolk sac infection!

When chicks die within a week of hatching, people will often jump to the wrong conclusions as to the cause. They scrub out their incubators, sterilise the room they use and clean everything they can but of course none of this helps because it is already too late.

Every year I have a few problems with bacteria getting into eggs from particular species such as penguins and spoonbills because their nest sites get dirty very quickly and cleaning them every few days would probably put the birds off laying. There is not much I can do about the occasional egg being lost in this way.

An example where I knew the nest site was the problem was when three European Spoonbill eggs came into the incubation room and were cleaned, sterilised and placed in an appropriate incubator. There were many other eggs in the same incubator. The spoonbill eggs were all fertile and had a normal weight loss during incubation of about 15%.

But within 48 hours of hatching they all died!

Post mortems on all three showed yolk sac infections and as none of the other eggs in the same incubator had problems during Incubation or after hatching, I could be fairly sure that there was not a problem in the incubator. The only conclusion I could come to was that the three spoonbill eggs picked up some bacteria when they were laid.

Obviously prevention is much better than cure so try and keep your nest sites as clean as possible. This is not normally a problem with birds like parrots but whatever type of eggs you are incubating it will occur occasionally.

If you do have an egg die during incubation, and results from sending it for a post mortem examination show a bacterial infection, don't automatically assume that it was from the nest site. It might have been but it is better to be "safe than sorry" so clean out your incubator anyway.

BEFORE YOU START

1.E Egg collecting

If you are collecting single eggs rather than clutches, try and collect them as soon as possible after laying so as to keep the risk of bacterial infection to a minimum.

When collecting eggs make sure you have something to carry them in like a clean bucket with a soft lining. Try not to carry them in your hands because if you fall over you will automatically open your hand to cushion your fall and that will be the end of your egg! If they are in a bucket with a soft lining the eggs will stand a bit more of a chance.

Be careful when taking the eggs from a nest site as sometimes the adult birds may suddenly attack and you may drop the eggs.

If the eggs are warm get them to an incubator quickly. An easy way to find out if the egg is warm or not is to place the egg on your eye lid as this is a very sensitive area of skin. If you can sense no temperature difference between the egg and your eye lid then the egg has been sat on so do not hang around.

Try not to check the nest site too often because this may put the hen off laying. Once you have had a pair of birds laying for a couple of years you will begin to understand their behavioural patterns and know when the hen is about to lay.

If you intend to replace the egg with a dummy egg, I suggest you warm the dummy egg up first because the hen may return to the nest fairly quickly after you leave and get a shock!

After collecting your eggs do not leave them at room temperature for too long a period. An egg will slowly start to develop at room temperature (70°F). This will kill the embryo if left too long or weaken it so that it dies some days later.

If you bring in an egg which is very cold, do not be afraid to leave it at room temperature for an hour or so before setting, in fact this can be a good idea as the egg will slowly warm up rather than suffer a sudden increase from very cold to incubation temperature. On the other hand leaving the egg at room temperature for more than a couple of hours would be dangerous.

PRACTICAL INCUBATION

1.F Handling an egg

If you don't achieve good success when incubating your eggs, buying better incubators and equipment may not help you. It could be something very easy to correct like the way you handle your eggs!

If you are turning your eggs by hand and jolt them, or when candling your eggs, you rotate them too fast, you may kill the developing embryo or damage it so that death occurs later.

When candling don't be too keen to see the first signs of growth because you may forget how long the egg has been out of the incubator.

A freshly laid egg is also delicate so take care when collecting, cleaning and marking it.

When you have got to candle a lot of eggs, do not be tempted to pick up more than one at a time as this will surely lead to accidents and for some unknown reason when an accident happens it is always with your most valuble egg!

If you are sterilising your eggs before you incubate them, the most important rule is never handle them again unless you have first scrubbed your hands very thoroughly in an anti-bacterial soap or hand wash.

You may think what I have written about the handling of eggs is just common sense ... it is! But this is where many eggs are lost and need not be.

1.G The incubation room

Most people will use a room in their own house. When choosing which room to use keep a few things in mind.

Try and pick a room which does not vary too much in temperature because even the most sophisticated and expensive incubators will vary slightly in temperature if the room varies in temperature.

This can be a big problem if, for example, you use a garden shed because when you visit the shed during the day, the temperature is fairly constant but at night it can drop by 10°C or more.

If you have to use a garden shed or out-building then a small heater with a thermostat will be enough to stop the temperature from varying too much.

A cellar is often a good choice as the temperature does not vary much at all, but make sure it is not too moist and that there is a good supply of fresh air.

Make sure you have plenty of plug sockets because nearly every piece of incubation equipment you buy is electrical.

Of course having surfaces in the incubation room which are easy to clean is a great help because this room will need to be kept spotless.

You can go a lot further and build an incubation room which is air conditioned, dehumidified, tiled, air filtered and sterilised, but of course you will need lot of money. The cost will outweigh the benefits for most people.

Many people use the same room as they use for rearing their chicks. This is not wrong as such but if you have a choice I would suggest you use a separate room because it will be easier to keep the incubators clean and sterile.

One other point to remember is to make sure that the room is vibration free. The occasional vibration is not important, but if you are next to a railway line or you put your incubator on a washing machine your eggs may have a few problems.

1.H Setting up and testing your incubator

It takes time and patience to set up an incubator. You cannot expect to switch on your incubator one day and use it the next.

Before the start of any breeding season, whether you are a beginner or have a good knowledge of incubators I suggest you turn your incubators on at least a month before you need them.

Each incubator seems to have its own personality and before you put your precious eggs into one, I suggest you learn exactly how it works and monitor it for as long as possible.

Before you turn your incubator on, and even if it was cleaned at the end of last season, I suggest you clean it now. It is a bit silly to get your incubator running smoothly and then turn it off to clean it before use because it may need adjusting again when you turn it back on.

Try and forecast what size eggs your birds are going to lay because nothing is more annoying than to suddenly find that you do not have the correct size tilting trays or rollers to suit your eggs. It would take several days for the incubator manufacturer to send new trays.

PRACTICAL INCUBATION

Testing your incubator is a good idea to make sure it works but probably just as important is that it gives you confidence in your incubator. The best way is to set the incubator up a couple of months before you need it and try to incubate some bantam eggs. These eggs are easy to incubate and it is better to practise on these eggs than your precious ones.

Also incubators behave differently when eggs are in them. Normally the more eggs in an incubator the more stable it becomes so you will learn how the incubator acts when it is full of eggs.

Another way to test your incubator is to place several thermometers in your incubator in different places. Beware because moving-air incubators and still-air incubators do vary in temperature depending on where you place the thermometer. If you don't take this into account it might remove any confidence you had in the incubator in the first place !!

A few guide lines before you start to test it with thermometers —

Firstly make sure all your thermometers agree with each other before you start. This can be simply done by placing them all into a lump of plasticine and comparing readings.

Secondly only place the thermometers on the same level as the eggs will be placed. There can be large temperature differences around the incubator but you are only interested in the temperature where the eggs will be placed.

The thermometer reading may go up and down slightly as you watch them. So a useful hint is to place a small lump of plasticine on the probe end of each thermometer, which will give the average temperature. Remember eggs take a long time to change temperature and it is the average temperature which is important. For example if an incubator varied from 37°C to 38°C every few minutes then it would still hatch eggs because the average temperature i.e. the temperature of the egg would be fairly constant at 37.5°C

If you have tested your incubator with several thermometers and hatched a few bantam eggs you should have some confidence in your machine. It seems to follow that the more confidence you have in your incubator the better results you will achieve.

Do not try and test more than one thing at a time in your incubator.

BEFORE YOU START

Clutch of Carolina Duck Eggs

African Spoonbill nest platform

Typical clean parrot nest

Penguin nest box

PRACTICAL INCUBATION

An easy and safe way to collect eggs

Eggs waiting to be processed

BEFORE YOU START

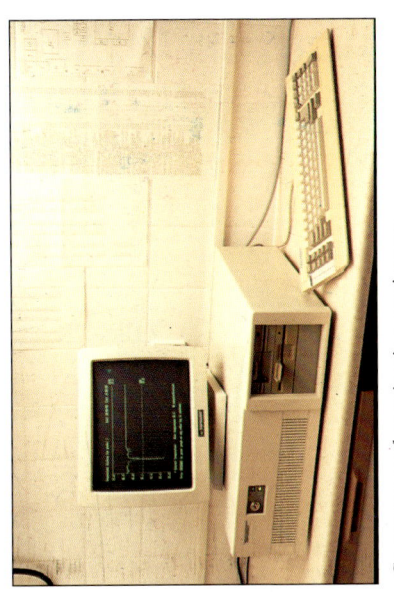

Computer and monitoring equipment

Dehumidifier

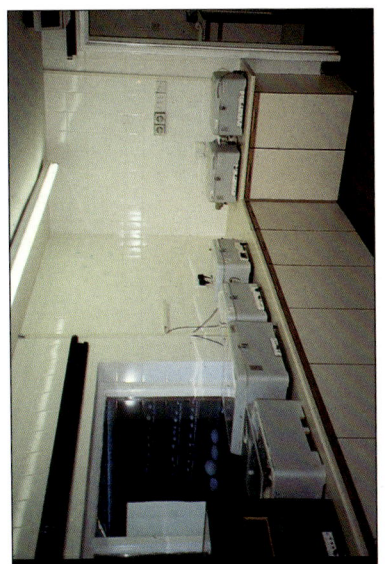

Incubators on easy to clean surfaces

Air conditioner

PRACTICAL INCUBATION

Check everything is clean before putting it all back together

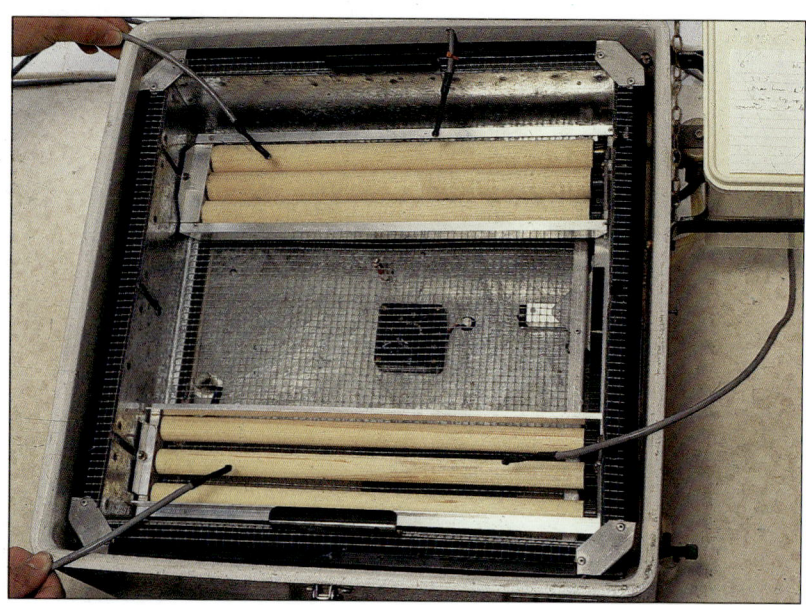

Testing an incubator bu using several themometers

14

BEFORE YOU START

Get the temperature constant in your incubator before you try and control the humidity or even turn on the automatic turning, if you have it.

When testing an incubator it is extremely useful to have pen and paper at hand. You can then write down the date, time and temperature each time you look at your incubator and then only adjust your incubator once a day. If you adjust the incubator slightly every time you look at it you may slowly go insane. If you adjust it after several readings have been taken, then you will be adjusting it in accordance with the average temperature and not one odd reading.

One thing to remember is that tilting trays in an incubator or any turning mechanism will alter the internal air flows and you may find the temperature reading on your thermometer varies at hourly intervals. This is not a problem as the average temperature is the only important temperature.

1.I Records

If you have a memory like mine then records are extremely important. I would suggest you keep accurate records of your incubator temperatures. If every time you walk into your incubation room you write down the temperature of your incubators you will see patterns appear of how the temperature varies at different times.

It is much safer to adjust your incubator by looking at the average from ten readings than from just one reading.

The graph on the following page Fig.1.1, is a typical example of how much the temperature fluctuates in a small incubator. The graph shows readings taken every three minutes over a 12 hour period.

Also if you record regular readings from your wet bulb thermometers and you start to get readings each time that are slightly higher than the last reading, this would probably mean that the wick is starting to get soiled and needs changing. By just glancing at the wet bulb thermometer each time you enter the incubation room you would not have noticed the slight changes in temperature.

One other advantage is that if an incubator goes wrong you can show the manufacturer how the incubator has been acting over a period of time and this could help him to find out what has caused the problem.

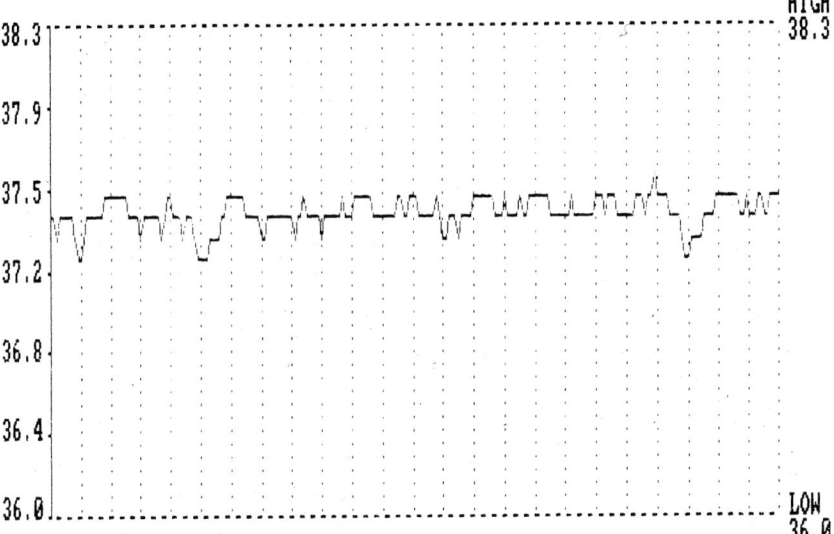

Fig 1.1; This graph shows temperature readings from a small 25 egg incubator over a period of 12 hours.

The most important records are of course the records from all the eggs that you have incubated.

When you are monitoring weight loss with your eggs it is very useful to know which pair of birds is likely to lay eggs that are very porous or thick shelled.

Having unrelated stock is of great importance in that the offspring will be much stronger and easier to raise. If you buy new stock try and find out where they came from originally and then write down in your records as much information as possible about each bird.

In a few years time you may start to expand your collection of birds and it will be difficult to remember exactly where they came from and, more importantly, if the new birds you are about to buy are related to your own.

2 Basic Incubation

2.A Hygiene

I have heard many people say "Why do we need to keep our incubators so clean when, in the wild, eggs are in nests which can be far from sterile".

If you are getting problems with eggs from a particular species of bird then making comparisons with how they are naturally incubated in the wild can be very useful indeed. But we cannot compare how hygienic the adult birds may be when incubating their eggs to how hygienic we must be when artificially incubating eggs.

There are two very good reasons for this. Firstly our incubators are often being used to incubate large numbers of eggs at any one time.

In the wild, with parrot eggs for example, there is one incubator for only three or four eggs. The chance of cross infection is very low because there are not many eggs in each incubator! In contrast, we may have 20 or 200 eggs in one incubator and if we get a nasty bug in the incubator then a large number of eggs could be lost. In the wild, if a nasty bug gets into a nest of parrot eggs then perhaps most of one clutch may be lost, but as so few eggs are in each clutch, only a couple of eggs will be lost.

Also, if a bird in the wild normally rears two chicks a year then it will lay more than two eggs just in case they don't all hatch. In captivity we have birds that are very rare (and also very expensive) so we do not want to risk losing any eggs during incubation as far as possible.

The second thing to remember is that in the wild the "incubator" is only going to be used for one clutch of eggs. So if the nest site is a bit dirty by the end of incubation it is not too important.

We may use an incubator for six months !

PRACTICAL INCUBATION

During this time, if you do not regularly sterilise your incubator, bacteria will slowly start to build up then your precious eggs will be at risk.

If you do not clean your incubation equipment regularly you may only lose a small percentage of eggs most years. But when a nasty bug does appear in an incubator you stand the chance of losing almost every single egg that it contains.

It is very common for eggs to pick up bacteria in an incubator and although it might not kill the developing chick then, the chances are it will kill it a week or so after hatching.

Obviously then it is a good idea to keep the incubation room and all equipment as clean as possible. I would suggest that the incubation room you are intending to use is given an extremely good clean before the season starts. Thereafter, incubators should be sterilised approximately every three weeks if possible.

In addition, if you can get into a regular routine every morning of wiping over the surfaces in the incubation room, and also anything you are likely to touch after you have scrubbed your hands, then this will help considerably in the fight against bacteria.

2.B Cleaning eggs

It is a complete waste of time to clean and sterilise your eggs if you handle them later at any time during incubation without properly scrubbing your hands first in an anti-bacterial soap or hand wash!

When you dip your eggs, hopefully you kill off any harmful bacteria. However if you handle your sterilised egg later without cleaning your hands, you will put a few bacteria back onto the egg shell. Remember that the temperature the egg is being incubated at is also the temperature that bacteria like best. So they will multiply very fast and possibly kill your developing embryo.

How to clean your eggs:

If there is any muck or dirt on the egg then remove it gently by scraping it off with a knife.

The next step is to dip your egg in one of the many brands of egg disinfectant on the market. If unsure which brand to use then go and

BASIC INCUBATION

see someone who is successfully hatching eggs and ask them what brand they use.

Whatever you do choose to dip your eggs in you must always make sure the water plus sterilising agent is much warmer than your egg. Because your egg is porous, when it is placed in a warmer liquid it will push out any bacteria in the pores of the egg shell which will then be killed by the sterilising agent. If the liquid is colder than the egg, when dipped the egg will suck in any bacteria in the pores of the egg shell and therefore the bacteria will not be destroyed.

I would suggest dipping the egg for only a few seconds only but rotate the egg in your fingers so that the whole of the egg shell comes in contact with the sterilising agent.

Your egg is now clean so do not put it down on an egg tray which has not been cleaned recently, or candle it on a candler which has just been used to candle a dirty egg, or in an incubator which has not been sterilised yet.

Do not dip too many eggs in one solution of egg dip because it soon cools and becomes less effective.

Stick to the instructions for the concentrations of the egg dip because too strong a solution may kill the embryo as well as bacteria on it!

Be careful when dipping your eggs because, as the cuticle which is on the outside of the shell becomes wet, it gets slippery and it is very easy to drop them.

There are other ways of sterilising your eggs like using U.V light but this light is very dangerous to human eyes and it is difficult to get the correct concentration of light on the eggs so I would not recommend it.

You can gas eggs in formaldehyde but it is extremely important to get the concentration correct because too much gas will kill the developing cells inside the egg. For most people dipping eggs is the safest method for both the egg and the person handling the egg!

Please do not forget that once the egg has been dipped it is clean so never touch it again without cleaning your hands first. I have mentioned this before but this is where many people make a fundamental mistake.

When scraping off muck or dipping an egg never have the blunt end pointing downward because this will strain the membranes inside the egg between the albumen and the air space.

Finally, as it can be time-consuming to keep weighing a very small amount of egg disinfectant it is a good idea to find a small scoop like a pen top which holds the small amount you require.

2.C Thermometers

Thermometers can be a real problem as there are so many types of them on the market. Most thermometers on the market are either mercury thermometers or digital thermometers. The main difficulty is to find a thermometer which is not only accurate but is CONSISTENTLY accurate. Just because a thermometer costs £25 or £40 does not necessarily mean it is accurate. Often you will find that they are consistently inaccurate. What I mean by this is that if they are reading two degrees low, then they will always read two degrees low.

I suggest you test all your thermometers before the start of every breeding season.

You will need to find a thermometer to compare yours with. Personally I have always used one particular thermometer for this purpose which I know to be accurate and against which I test all the other thermometers I use.

I acquired ten digital thermometers. Of these, six were within $0.2^{\circ}C$ of my "accurate thermometer" so I now use these for hatching purposes.

For the person who has just acquired a thermometer, the best way to test it is to take it to somebody who is hatching eggs at the moment and compare it to their thermometer. Be careful when comparing thermometers. If they are in an incubator within an inch of each other the temperature could differ by up to half a degree fahrenheit in that short distance!

So to stop you going insane, which can easily happen when testing thermometers, I suggest you push the probes of the thermometers into the centre of a small lump of plasticine. Then put thermometers and plasticine into an incubator for an hour or so. Because the plasticine is fairly dense the temperature of it tends to be even throughout and the actual temperature where the probes are should be the same for all of them.

BASIC INCUBATION

Probably the only real way to find out if your thermometer is accurate is to go to your local university and compare your thermometer to a "National Standards Quartz Thermometer".

Some people prefer digital thermometers, some prefer mercury thermometers. As far as accuracy is concerned there is not much in it but digital thermometers are easier to read and often have alarms on them which can be very useful. Don't fall into the trap which many people do of believing that just because they are digital thermometers they must be accurate. Some digital thermometers are not very accurate at all!

Once you are sure your thermometer is accurate, or you know it is reading a set amount high or low, it can be put to use.

The next step is to decide where to place it in the incubator. Where the manufacturers suggest you put the thermometer may be the obvious place, but is not always the best place.

Personally I put my thermometers about one and a half inches above the eggs, near the centre of the incubator. This is for a moving-air incubator. In a still-air incubator you must be more precise in placing your thermometer. It should be on the same level as the eggs because of the large temperature gradient between the top of the incubator and the bottom.

Do not put the thermometer right next to an egg because this can give a false reading if the egg has just been put in or if the egg is close to hatching (eggs give out heat when close to hatching).

If you are hatching eggs successfully and your thermometer is on the edge of the incubator or wherever, do not move it - leave well alone!!

2.D Wet bulb thermometers

Wet bulb thermometers and relative humidity seem to cause more confusion than anything else in incubation.

First of all you need to understand how a wet bulb thermometer works. There is nothing special about the thermometer at all, it is an ordinary thermometer with a piece of wick attached to the end of it. This wick is continuously supplied with water to keep it wet. The wet bulb thermometer works on a very simple principal: as water evaporates from the wick the thermometer is cooled. So if a lot of water is evaporating from the wick the thermometer will have a low reading and if hardly any water is being evaporated from the wick then the thermometer will have a high reading.

Let's assume we have a very dry incubator. In this incubator the air that passes the wet bulb is very dry so will pick up a lot of water from the wick and therefore cool the thermometer considerably and you will have a low reading.

If on the other hand we assume we have a very wet incubator then the air which passes the wick is already very moist so it will take up hardly any water. Therefore the thermometer will give us a high reading as it is not being cooled very much.

You can convert the readings on the wet bulb thermometer to relative humidity by using the table on page 117.

However for most people relative humidity is irrelevant because if the dry bulb reading is constant, which it will be in your incubator, then the humidity is directly proportional to the wet bulb reading.

If the dry bulb reading is constant, and nearly all makes of incubator keep a good constant temperature nowadays, then the following is true:

THE HIGHER THE READING ON A WET BULB THERMOMETER, THE HIGHER THE HUMIDITY IN THE INCUBATOR.

THE LOWER THE READING ON A WET BULB THERMOMETER THE LOWER THE HUMIDITY IN THE INCUBATOR.

Problems with wet bulbs:

Soiled Wicks.

As water evaporates from the wick of a wet bulb thermometer it will leave behind anything else which is in the water. So after a period of time the wick becomes soiled and gives you a false reading.

Using distilled water will help but after approximately three weeks the wick will need changing or washing.

What happens when the wick becomes soiled is that the residue

BASIC INCUBATION

that has built up on the wick decreases the area that water can evaporate from. This gives you a false reading which is higher than it should be. Therefore the incubator will be drier than the reading on the wet bulb indicates.

If you decide to use a small amount of disinfectant in the water reservoir which feeds the wick then the wick will become soiled much quicker and will need changing more often, but nevertheless this is of course a good idea to stop a bacteria build-up in the water.

It is easy to see when a wick needs changing because it can become discoloured and it feels slimy to the touch. To avoid this problem I would suggest changing or washing the wick at least every two weeks.

Also if the temperature on the wet bulb increases a bit every day then this means the wick is getting soiled, so change it. If a sudden increase in temperature is seen on the wet bulb thermometer then either the wick has run dry because you have not added water recently or the wick has slipped off the thermometer.

If you are installing a wet bulb thermometer in an incubator make sure the distance between the thermometer and the water reservoir is about one inch. If the distance is too far then most of the water will have evaporated from the wick before it reaches the thermometer and you will get a false high reading.

Try and clean out the water reservoir every few weeks as this is a place which bacteria seem to like.

If you get information from someone who is hatching eggs of a species in which you are interested and they do not add water to their incubator, then this does not necessarily mean that you need not add water to your incubator. You may live in a drier area so will need to add water. To find out if you do need to add water simply find out the wet bulb reading on their incubator and keep yours the same.

The sensors on incubators with automatic humidity control use wicks in the same way as has been described above so keep them clean as well. If the wick on the sensor gets soiled the incubator will believe the correct humidity has been achieved but in fact it is too dry.

There are other ways of measuring humidity in incubators, like the hair hygrometer for example, but these are often very inaccurate indeed. The humidity can be measured electronically but this method, although accurate, is extremely costly.

PRACTICAL INCUBATION

You can add automatic humidity controls to any incubator if they don't have them, which is much cheaper than buying a complete new incubator which does. The people who sell these add-on humidity controls will advise you where to place the sensor and wet bulb in your incubator

Wet bulbs are essential if you intend to use weight loss techniques with your precious eggs.

2.E Moving-air incubators

A moving-air incubator is simply an incubator which has a fan in it to move the air around.

The air in a moving-air incubator has a fairly constant temperature throughout the machine. This does not mean you can place your thermometer anywhere in the incubator. The temperature could be a degree higher near the heating element for instance, but in general the temperature remains fairly constant throughout the incubator compared to a still-air incubator which is not fan assisted.

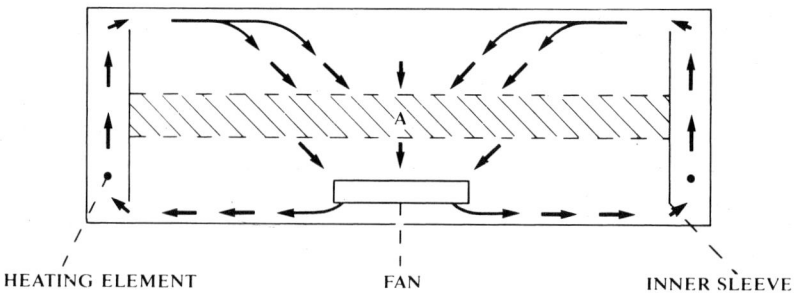

A   = AREA WHERE EGGS SIT
➤ = AIR FLOW

Diagram.2.1; Cross section of a typical moving air incubator

24

BASIC INCUBATION

As you can see in diagram 2.1 the air is being forced from the fan across the bottom of the incubator and then up the sides.

The heating element is normally on the side of the incubator between the outer wall and an inner sleeve. This is done for safety reasons so you cannot touch the heating element during normal use. In some incubators the element is at the top or bottom of the incubator but always in a place that it is difficult to touch it by accident.

So the air in the incubator is flowing in a circle, from the fan across the bottom, up the side past the heater and then down over the eggs to the fan again.

Automatic turning can affect the air flow and therefore can cause hot and cold spots.

Every moving air incubator on the market varies slightly in how the air flows around the machine.

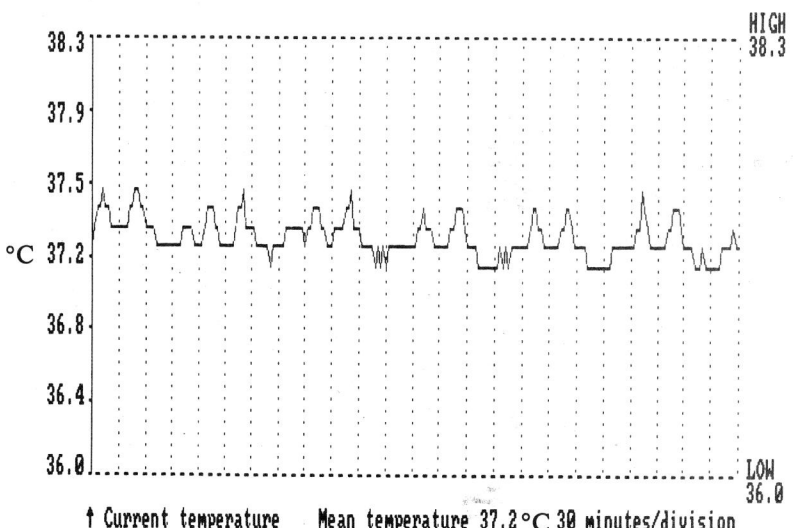

Fig 2.1; This graph shows temperature readings from a 80 egg incubator over a period of 12 hours.

PRACTICAL INCUBATION

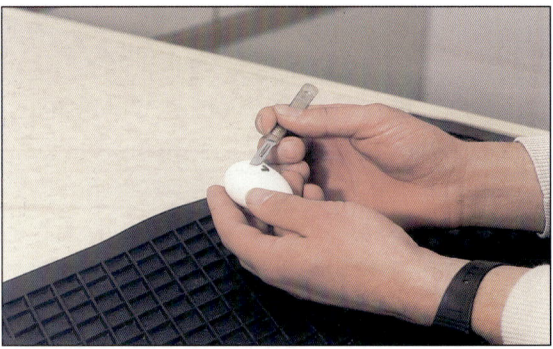

Carefully removing any dirt or muck from an egg

Dipping an egg to sterlise it

Leaving eggs to dry before placing them in an incubator

PRACTICAL INCUBATION

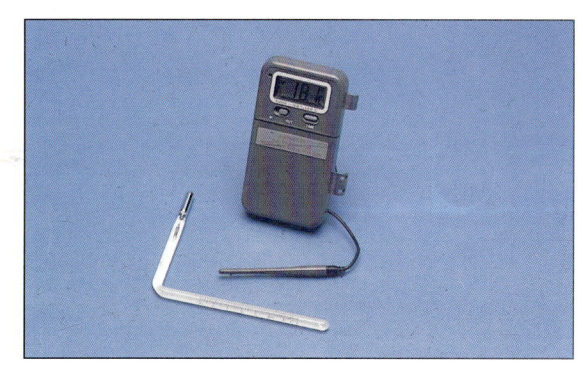

Two common types of thermometers mercury and digital

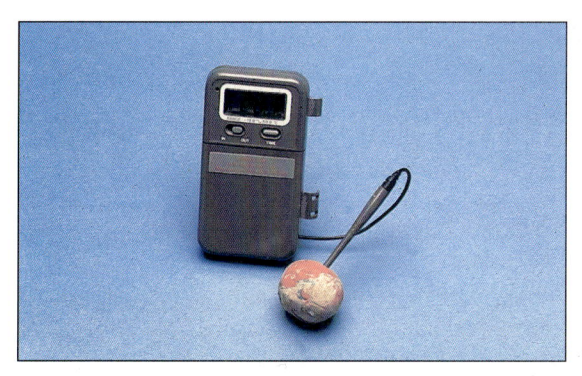

Using plasticine to find the average temperature

Where to place a thermometer in a still air incubator

PRACTICAL INCUBATION

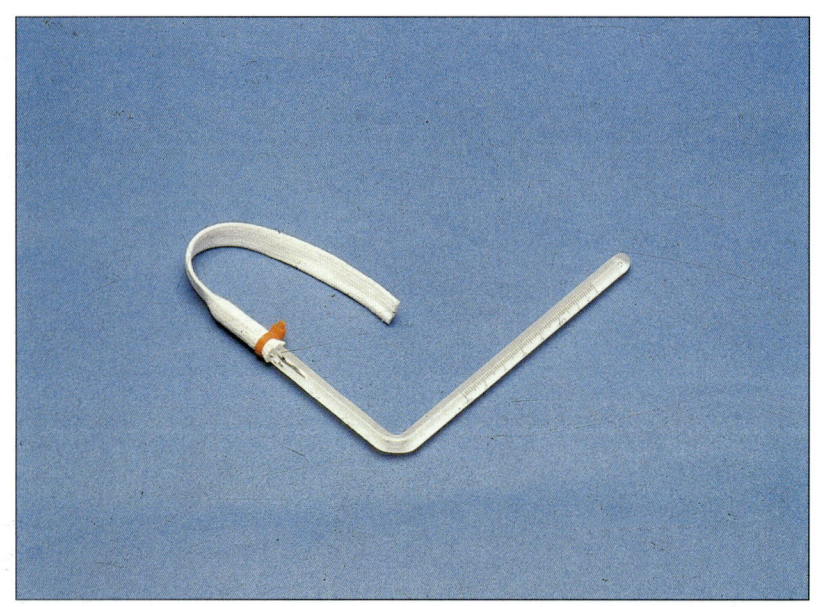

A wet bulb thermometer

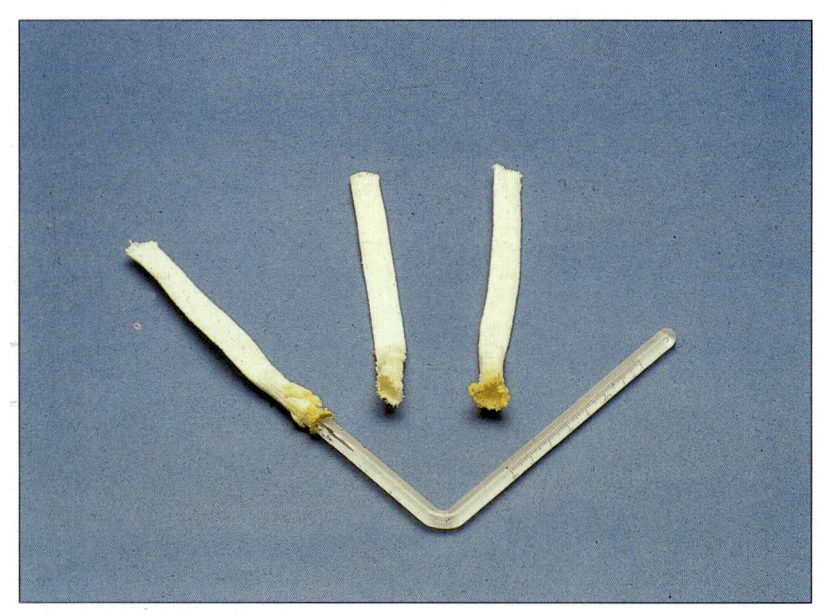

Bad or soiled wicks

28

BASIC INCUBATION

Eggs being turned on tilting trays

Eggs being turned on a moving carpet incubator

Turning eggs by hand

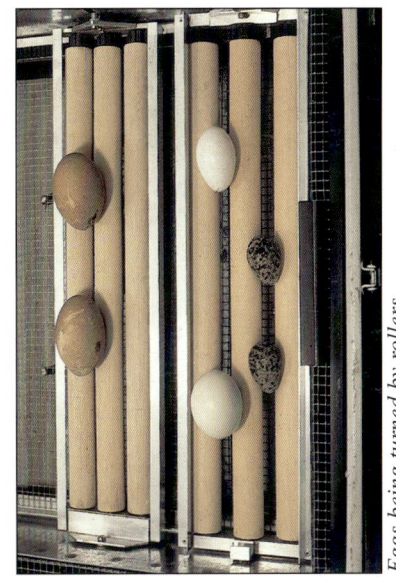

Eggs being turned by rollers

29

PRACTICAL INCUBATION

Changing the wick on a wet bulb thermometer

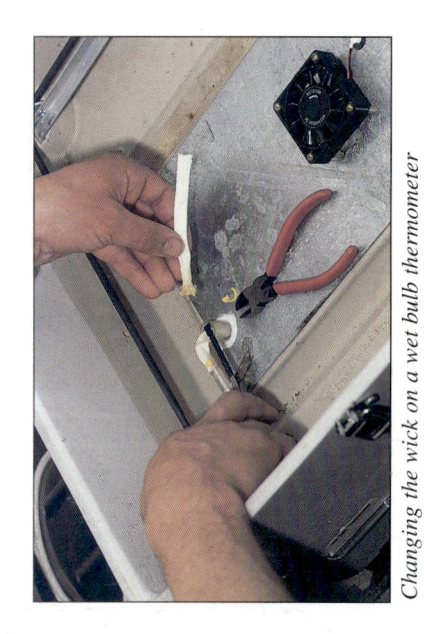

A Gassing Dish

Wiping over the shell of the incubator

Parts of an Incubator being scubbed

BASIC INCUBATION

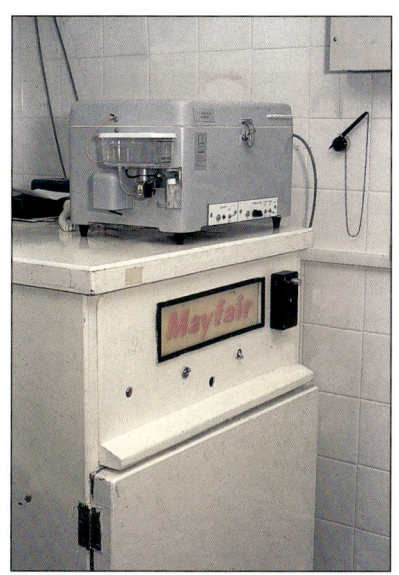

A typical incubator that has been converted to use electronic temperature components.

Chicks hatching in a large incubator

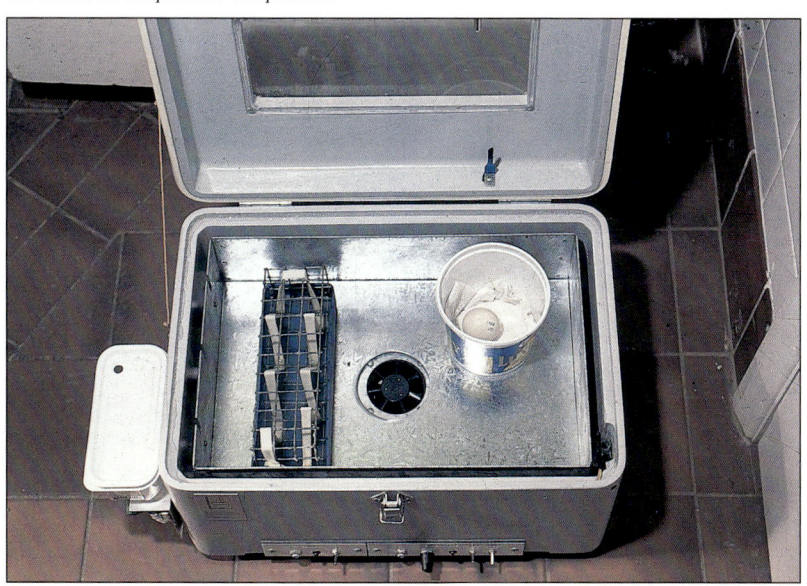

A small incubator used as a hatcher

PRACTICAL INCUBATION

It used to be the case that the larger the incubator the more constant the temperature. Fortunately small incubators have advanced enormously in recent years.

The three temperature graphs are from different size incubators.

The first graph, Fig. 1.1. I would like you to look at is from a very small 25 egg incubator. This graph is on page 16.

This graph shows readings taken every three minutes over a 12 hour period. As you can see the temperature is only varying by 3°C which is excellent.

The second graph, Fig.2.1, on page 25 was taken from an incubator that would hold approx 80 eggs is again only varying by 0.3°C

When people say this incubator is a 80 egg or a 600 egg incubator they mean that it would hold approximately that number of bantam eggs.

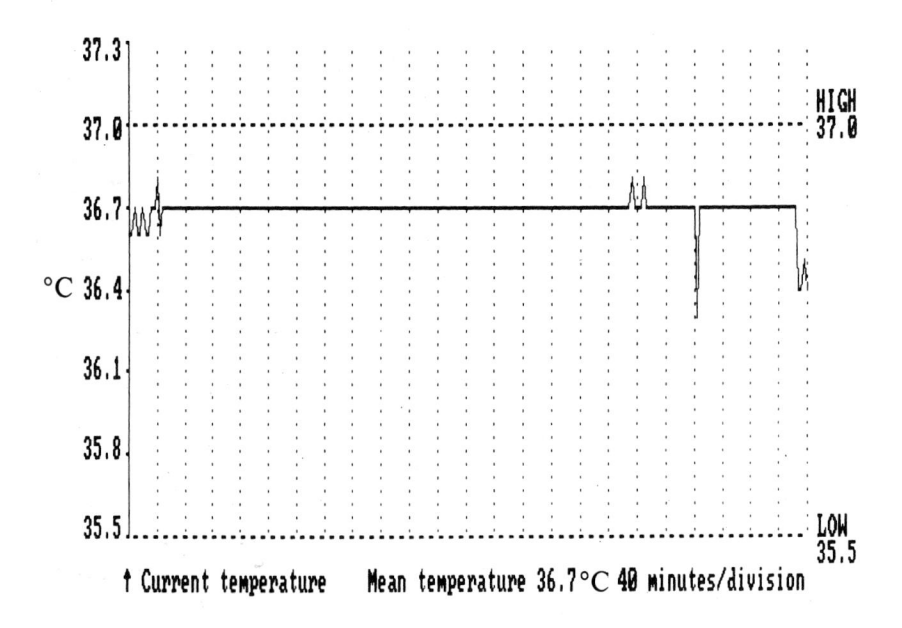

↑ Current temperature   Mean temperature 36.7°C 40 minutes/division

Fig 2.2; This graph shows temperature readings from a 600 egg incubator over a 16 hour period

BASIC INCUBATION

The third graph, Fig.2.2, shows readings taken every four minutes over a 16 hour period. This is from a 600 egg incubator and as you can see it hardly varies in temperature at all. There is one 3°C blip on the right hand side but this was produced when the door was opened.

So you can see that very large incubators are more constant in temperature but the point I am trying to get across is that an egg would be happy in any incubator with such small temperature variations.

One thing to remember is that these readings were taken from incubators in a room where the temperature does not vary more than 2°C. If you have a room that varies more than 4 or 5 you would not get such good graphs as these. For advice on the incubation room see section 1 chapter on The Incubation Room.

2.F Still-air incubators

The air in still-air incubators does move but only very slowly. The incubator is relying on the air being moved round by convection.

Any air near the heating element rises as it warms up so a circular air flow is produced not unlike the air flow in a moving-air incubator. But of course, as it is not fan-assisted, it is much slower.

The main problem with still-air incubators is that there is a large temperature gradient from the top to the bottom of the incubator, as much as 5°C in some incubators! This is not too much of a problem as long as the eggs are at the correct temperature. If your eggs are at 37°C for example, it might be 39°C at the top of the incubator and as low as 35°C at the bottom. As you can imagine if you put a thermometer at the top of the incubator and adjust the temperature to 37.5°C . Then your eggs will only be 36°C .

This is where many people get confused with still-air machines. Often the manufacturer will have the thermometer at the top of the machine and tell you to incubate your eggs at a temperature that seems too high. But the manufacturers have done extensive tests and know how much the temperature differs from where the thermometer is compared to where you will place your eggs.

It is easier for the manufacturer to place the thermometer at the top of the incubator. If you are going to place a thermometer in a still-air incubator then the best place to put it is on the same level as

BASIC INCUBATION

the eggs and if possible on a level that is midway between the top and bottom of the eggs

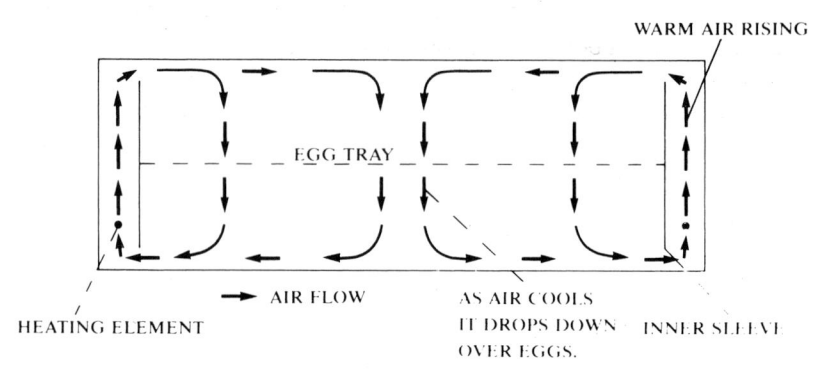

Diagram. 2.2. Showing the air flow in a still incubator

You cannot have large still-air incubators because only one level in the incubator has the correct temperature. With a moving air incubator there can be several levels which have the same temperature.

The following graph, Fig 2.3, shows readings taken every three minutes over a 16 hour period from a still air incubator

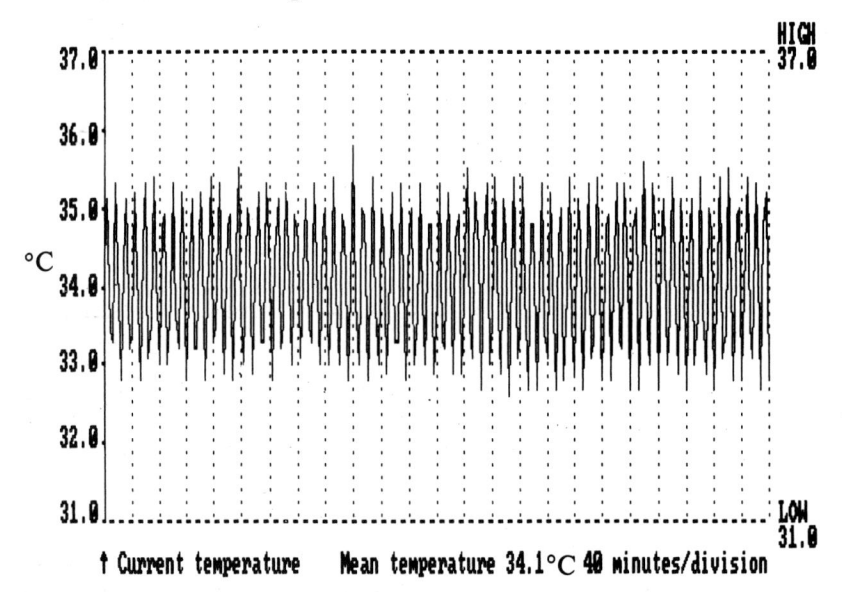

Fig 2.3. This graph shows temperature readings from a typical still air incubator over a period of 16 hours.

BASIC INCUBATION

Be very careful if you are comparing the temperature of a still-air incubator to a moving-air incubator. You must measure the temperature of the still-air incubator at the level where the eggs are and at a mid point between the top and bottom of the eggs that you are incubating.

This can be difficult if you incubate different size eggs in the same incubator. For example if you incubate an ostrich egg and a quail egg in the same still air incubator then the eggs will be incubated at different temperatures!

The mid-point of the ostrich egg is its average incubation temperature. But the quail egg is rather small compared to an ostrich and its mid point is a couple of inches lower and therefore 1 or 2°C lower in temperature. So two eggs in the same machine can end up being incubated at different temperatures.

This example is an extreme and I realise that no one would normally incubate an ostrich egg and quail egg together but it is a good way of explaining the temperature variation in a still-air incubator.

For a beginner at incubation I would suggest that you go for a moving air incubator as they are easier to use.

One other thing to mention is that if you are getting good results with a still air incubator, don't change!!!

This is because you will have confidence in your incubator and that helps to get good results.

2.G Turning eggs

There are several methods that are used in incubators to turn eggs automatically. They are tilting trays, rollers, moving carpet and a moving grid system. Of course many people turn eggs by hand.

It is true that if you have a 100 bantam eggs that are not turned at all during incubation, Approximately 50 of them will hatch. This suggests that turning of eggs is not that important but I'm afraid turning has got to be very precise indeed with exotic eggs.

I used to use tilting trays for all my eggs with the exception of eggs from ostriches and rheas which I turned by hand. I now know that this is not good enough for many species of birds eggs.

PRACTICAL INCUBATION

The easiest way to explain this is to tell you what happened to me. On candling my eggs I noticed that all species of eggs should have complete vein growth by the time 60% of the incubation period has passed. What I mean by complete vein growth is that when you candle the egg you can see that veins are covering the whole egg.

Certain eggs which were being incubated seemed to be having problems. These eggs were macaw eggs, spoonbill eggs and night heron eggs. A very low percentage of these eggs hatched and all of them had some egg white left in the egg shell at hatch.

After some time I ruled out that perhaps I was incubating at a wrong temperature and I knew the weight loss was correct so I looked at the turning.

This is what I found. Of ten macaw eggs incubated on tilting trays that take one hour to slowly turn from one side to the other none seemed to develop properly and only one hatched. The next two clutches of macaw eggs were laid on their side and turned by hand seven times a day. They all had complete vein growth by day 14 and all hatched! The same results were obtained when other eggs from spoonbills and night herons were tried on their side.

So what I had discovered was that, whilst most eggs could go into tilting trays and would develop properly and hatch. Eggs from some species had to be incubated on their side. If the eggs from these problem species were incubated on rollers or moving carpets (i.e. the eggs were on their side) then they hatched.

So I had solved the problem of how to incubate these eggs but why did they need different turning during incubation compared to eggs from other species?

Well they all had one thing in common which was that the yolk of these eggs was very small! Perhaps because these eggs have small yolks and therefore a lot of white compared to other eggs the developing chick has a lot of white to absorb so more precise turning is needed to enable them to do this. I have spoken to many people about this and no one knows exactly why they need turning differently.

The main thing is that by candling regularly we can soon see if different turning is required. For monitoring eggs by candling see section 3 page 43.

A question now arises which is this : Would the eggs from species

BASIC INCUBATION

that hatch quite happily when incubated on tilting trays be even better off on their side ?? I do not know.

Once sixty percent of the incubation period has passed and you have complete vein growth then all eggs can be put into tilting trays with out adverse affect.

Some manufacturers of incubators now sell their machines so that you can have tilting trays or rollers in them or both.

Be careful when you use rollers because you will need different sized rollers for different sized eggs. For example, if a bantam egg rotates $180°$ on a roller then on the same roller a goose egg would only rotate approximately $90°$ because it is so much larger. This would not be enough turning for it to develop properly.

There are eggs from some species that still seem to be difficult to incubate but soon I think there will be some interesting results from my Incubation Research Station at Birdworld. As soon as there are they will be published.

2.H How to clean your incubator

Electronics and water do not mix very well. I have been to several incubator manufacturers and seen their graveyards of incubators sent back after the owners had cleaned them and then turned the incubator back on only for them to blow up !

Incubators do need cleaning regularly during the egg laying season. Although an incubator may still look clean several weeks after you last cleaned it, do not forget that however much you have cleaned an egg before placing it in an incubator, it is possible for an egg to acquire bacteria as it is laid. So you may add the occasional egg to your incubator which will spread bacteria around the machine. If the incubator is spotlessly clean then you will have a good chance that the bacteria will not build up too much to harm your other eggs.

Gasing an incubator using formaldehyde gas is the best way to ensure that the incubator is as free from bacteria as possible.

It is a waste of time gasing your incubator with formaldehyde if you have not removed any shell, droppings etc first. This is because, if you have a piece of shell on the bottom of the incubator when you gas it, then all the bacteria on top of the shell will be destroyed but

PRACTICAL INCUBATION

not any bacteria which are underneath the shell. So before you think of gasing an incubator I would suggest that you remove egg trays and anything else that can be removed and thoroughly scrub them in a sink.

Many incubators are built nowadays so that not only the egg trays are removable but also the turning gear and sometimes the inner shell of the incubator as well, so all these bits will be easy to scrub down.

What you are left with is the part of an incubator which has electronics in it. Do not dump this bit into a sink to clean it !

The best thing to do is to gently wipe over the remaining part of the incubator with a disinfectant on the market recommended for cleaning incubators.

Once the incubator plus all the innards have dried then put it back together. Now is the time to gas your incubator and the easiest way to do this is to buy a small heater dish and some "formaldehyde" crystals from your local garden centre.

Please remember that only a very small amount of powder is required to gas an incubator. On the packet it will recommend something like a tea spoon of powder for 10,000 cubic feet. Your incubator might only be 2 cubic feet!

When you start to gas your incubator be careful that you do not gas yourself!

It is best to leave your incubator for an hour or so after the powder has vapourised, this way most of the gas will have dispersed before you open the door. Make sure that the room that you are in has very good ventilation before you start.

You can clean an incubator by just wiping over all the surfaces with a good disinfectant but you will not reach every single bit of the incubator. When you gas an incubator switch the incubator on and this will ensure that the formaldehyde gas reaches every nook and cranny.

Your incubator has now been sterilised so treat it as such. Do not handle the egg trays or any part in the incubator without first cleaning your hands with an anti-bacterial soap or handwash. Your hands may look clean but there will be millions of bacteria on them until they are washed properly.

During the incubation season I would suggest that you clean your incubator at least every three weeks if that is possible.

BASIC INCUBATION

The incubator that you use for hatching must be cleaned regularly. Hatchers are warm and humid, perfect conditions for bacteria! After just one egg has hatched there are small pieces of egg shell, possibly a dropping of two, some fluff from the chick as it dries and of course the remains of the egg itself. As you can imagine these make good breeding grounds for bacteria. So the best thing to do if possible is to clean out the hatcher after each egg has hatched or each group of eggs have hatched.

A good idea is to have small plastic margarine tubs in the hatcher into which you can put the eggs which are hatching so that any droppings or small pieces of shell will be contained. Then the cleaning of the incubator will be made easier.

Finally to help keep the bacteria down to a minimum it is a good idea to add a small amount of disinfectant to the water which is being used to keep the humidity high in the hatcher.

2.1 Hatching Incubators

You must have a separate incubator for hatching eggs, even if you only have a few eggs to hatch.

Your incubator that is used for hatching eggs must be very humid indeed. This is because you are trying to stop the chick from drying up whilst it is still in the egg. The chick has to be able to rotate inside the egg if it is to break the egg shell all the way round. If the air around the egg is very dry when it pips then the chick will start to dry and get very sticky. It will then not be able to rotate and therefore will need assistance to hatch or end up "dead in shell ".

Once the chick has broken the egg shell all around the egg, it pushes its way out from the shell. This is a critical time. The chick has to push hard to break the outer and inner membranes which are just inside the egg shell. These membranes are easy to break if moist but if allowed to dry they become very tough indeed and the chick will have no chance of hatching.

It is possible to kill a chick that is about to hatch if you open the incubator at the time that the chick is about break the membranes. At this point the chick is almost exhausted and if it has to struggle with membranes that have become tough then that could be fatal!

PRACTICAL INCUBATION

Both still-air incubators and moving-air incubators can be used as hatchers.

In both types of incubators there has to be a large area of water in the bottom of the incubator to produce very humid conditions.

In a still-air hatching incubator, after you have introduced an egg it will take a long time for the incubator to reach maximum humidity as the air inside is moving very slowly. This can become a problem if you are going to be adding eggs several times a day or you are a very impatient person that keeps on looking at your eggs as they are hatching! If you are an impatient person then try and get a still-air hatcher with a clear lid so you do not have to open the incubator to look at your eggs.

If you are going to be hatching a lot of eggs and can afford one, then I suggest you go for a moving-air incubator. The main reason for this is that once the door of the incubator is closed the air inside becomes very humid indeed in a short time. This is because the air is being forced over the water in the incubator. Therefore, the air will pick up moisture much quicker than in a still-air incubator.

I like my eggs which are hatching to be in air that is not moving too fast but I must have my eggs in a moving-air hatcher because I am adding eggs several times a day. The solution I have found is to use a moving-air incubator for hatching eggs but place the eggs in plastic tubs. Once the door is closed, I know maximum humidity will be reached very quickly and the eggs do not have air rushing past them.

Eggs start to produce some heat a few days before they hatch so to stop them over-heating, the incubator that you use for hatching your eggs in should be about 1°C lower than the temperature that you have incubated them in so far.

Incubators used as hatchers get dirty very quickly indeed. After only a few eggs have hatched there will be pieces of shell, dust and fine fluff from the chick as it dries. So I would suggest you sterilise the hatcher as often as you can.

If you are hatching large numbers of eggs then it it advisable to have two hatchers so that you can clean one hatcher every day by simply putting the eggs in the other.

Plastic tubs are also a good idea to help keep the hatcher clean because they stop any pieces of shell etc. from falling through the egg tray.

BASIC INCUBATION

For more information on problems when hatching eggs see the chapter on " hatching time " page 78.

2.J Good stock

If you do not have good adult stock then you will not get good results from incubating eggs either naturally, or artificially, however good at incubation you are!

There are many species of birds of which only a few pairs originally came into the country. As you can imagine to get birds of these species which are unrelated is very difficult.

Even if you get your male and female from different sources there are no guarantees that they are not related. Also many people keep one pair of a species and breed from them. They might then sell a young pair to another breeder who should try and swap one of the birds for new blood. But often people find this difficult and decide that first generation brother and sister can't do any harm. It might not, but the trouble is this can then go on through succeeding generations and the birds get weaker and weaker.

Birds that are very related are very weak specimens which produce eggs that are of poor quality and difficult to incubate. If you do manage to incubate the eggs then you end up with weak chicks that are difficult to rear. Also very related birds can produce deformed chicks.

So, to obtain good results in incubation and rearing of young birds make sure your adult stock is as unrelated as possible !

If we all had no choice of our partners then I am sure that the human race would be a lot smaller than it is today as some of us might not like each other!! The point I am making is that just because you buy a male and female of the same species does not mean that they will breed or even like each other.

Many successful breeders will buy ten birds of a new species and from them hope to get 2 or 3 compatible pairs. They will then sell the rest. Some parrot breeders will put ten birds together in a large flight so that they can choose their own partners. You will get more compatible pairs by this method but before you all rush out to try this be aware that you also can get a lot of fighting!

PRACTICAL INCUBATION

By good stock we mean birds that are unrelated and compatible but also they must be well kept. If fed on the wrong diet they might look all right but produce eggs that even if fertile do not hatch. There is no way the adult bird can put the correct vitamins and trace elements etc into an egg if they are not getting them in the first place! If you concentrate on getting good unrelated stock that are compatible and correctly looked after, then incubating their eggs will be much more successful.

3 Monitoring Your Eggs

3.A Candling

There is much more to candling than just finding out if the egg is fertile or not.

There are many people who use weight loss techniques and even density loss techniques to monitor their eggs but seem to neglect the most important way of monitoring an egg's progress which is candling. By candling your eggs regularly you can see the growth of the embryo increase almost every day.

After some practice at candling eggs you will learn by experience what they should look like when developing correctly and you will also know if something goes wrong. If the development differs from what you have seen before then this can point to problems with temperature, humidity or turning.

First of all you will need a strong light to candle your eggs with and there are many types for sale which will do most eggs. If you have eggs like some of the ones I have at Birdworld e.g ostrich, cranes, storks, penguins etc. then a very strong light will be necessary. Often a slide projector light is the best to use.

With parrot eggs it is not a problem because a 40 watt light bulb in a box with a small hole in it is all that is required because the egg shells are very easy to see through. Be careful the box does not over heat and cook your eggs while you candle them !

The quickest way to become proficient at candling is to go and see someone who has been candling eggs for years and can pass on her or his experience.

A suggestion for the beginner, or anybody regularly candling eggs, is to candle your eggs at least every other day and write down exactly

PRACTICAL INCUBATION

what you see. The easiest thing to see is the amount of growth so far, e.g. the embryo now covers 50% of the egg or 80% of the egg or whatever. It is impossible for me to remember exactly what each egg I candle looked like last time I candled it so writing it down is the only way if your memory is like mine.

Also if you candle your eggs regularly and notice there has not been any increase in the size of the embryo over a period of four days (for an incubation period of 21 days) and the embryo is still alive then that would probably point to a turning problem.

When candling a precious egg be careful you don't overlook how long you have been candling it. You may chill it or, if your candler gets hot, cook it!

Be careful not to rotate your eggs too fast on the candler because this could damage a membrane inside the egg and kill the developing embryo. Though it might not kill the embryo straight away, it could weaken it so that it dies later.

Initially candling is usually done at the blunt end of the egg but once the embryo is more than a week old you will be able to see much more by candling it at the sharp end. In fact from the middle to near the end of incubation the best place to candle the egg is at the sharp end.

The following graph, Fig. 3.1, can be used as a guide when candling eggs. This graph shows the development of Vulturine Guinea Fowl eggs as seen from candling them.

The line on the graph is drawn from day 4 to day $13\frac{1}{2}$. This is because the first sign of growth is seen on day 4 and on day 13/14 there are veins covering all of the egg. The graph shows the average growth rate of the veins in Vulturine Guinea Fowl eggs.

As you can see there is rapid growth from day 4 to day 8. Then for a couple of days when you candle your eggs you will see hardly any more vein growth. This is nothing to worry about because it happens to all the eggs. Complete growth as far as candling is concerned is not complete development of the embryo.

Once complete growth is seen by candling then it is difficult to see further changes by candling.

The graph can be used as a guide for any species of birds eggs. With vulturine Guinea Fowl day $13\frac{1}{2}$ is 54% of the incubation

PRACTICAL INCUBATION

VULTURINE GUINEA FOWL

DAYS / % OF COVERED BY VEINS
AVERAGE FROM 21 EGGS

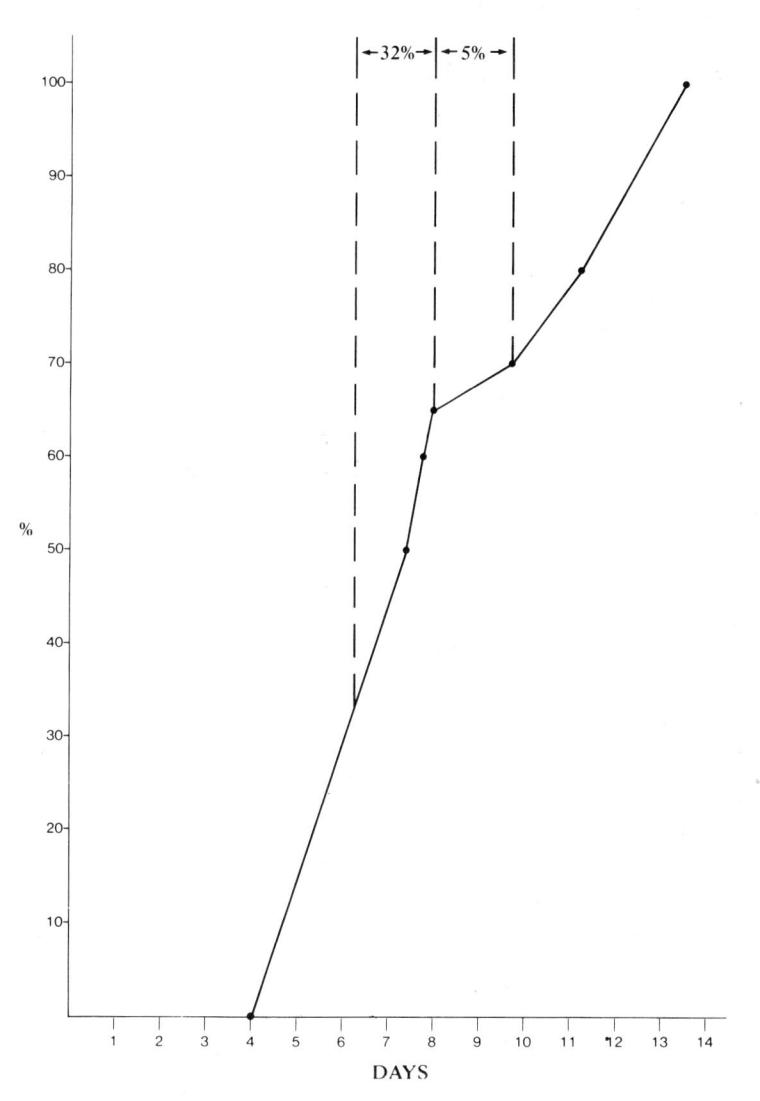

Fig 3.1; This graph shows percentage of vein growth covering the egg shell surface against days of incubation for an average of 21 Vulturine guinea fowl eggs

period. You will find that as long as your eggs are being incubated at the correct temperature and are being turned properly then you should get complete vein growth when approx 54% of the incubation period has passed. So as you can see this graph is very useful indeed as a guide to whether your eggs are being incubated correctly.

The best way to monitor your eggs is by using candling and weight loss or density loss techniques together.

3.B Weight loss techniques

During incubation eggs lose weight, approximately 20% of their laying weight. With weight loss techniques we are only interested in the weight loss from the start of incubation to when the egg internally pips. This is approximately 15% for all species.

What we mean by " internal pip " is when the chick breaks into the air space. The chick has not broken the egg shell yet but is starting to breathe the air in the air space. After the chick has internally pipped the weight loss increases and from this point to actually hatching the egg can lose another 5% to 10% of the laying weight.

The graph on page 47 is a typical weight loss graph showing a steady decrease in weight until the chick internally pips. After internally pipping the weight loss increases dramatically as shown.

For optimum results we need to monitor the weight loss of every single egg that we incubate.

It is wrong to presume that all eggs from one particular species will need the same humidity in an incubator. Maybe you could do this for eggs laid in the wild but for birds kept in captivity it does not work. The reason for this is that every person feeds their captive birds slightly differently, therefore the eggs that are laid can vary significantly. Even if you feed the same diet as the next person you will often find that one particular pair of birds lays odd eggs. To put this in perspective, we can say that on average one particular species needs humidity X but to achieve optimum results we must treat every egg as an individual. Because some species of birds are now very rare, very expensi-ve or both, hatching 7 or 8 out of ten is not good enough. We must go for 9 or 10 out of ten.

MONITORING YOUR EGGS

Another point to remember is that in your incubation room you could be incubating eggs from birds that normally live in a desert so most of these eggs would probably need an incubator with low humidity. In addition, you may have eggs from birds which would normally have lived in a tropical rain forest where the air is very humid and these eggs would probably need an incubator with high humidity. As you can see, to select precisely the humidity required for a given egg is both difficult and critical if we are to achieve maximum success. Weight loss of an egg is controlled by raising or lowering the humidity in an incubator.

If an egg is losing too much weight (ie too much moisture) then, by increasing the amount of water in the air around the egg, we can slow

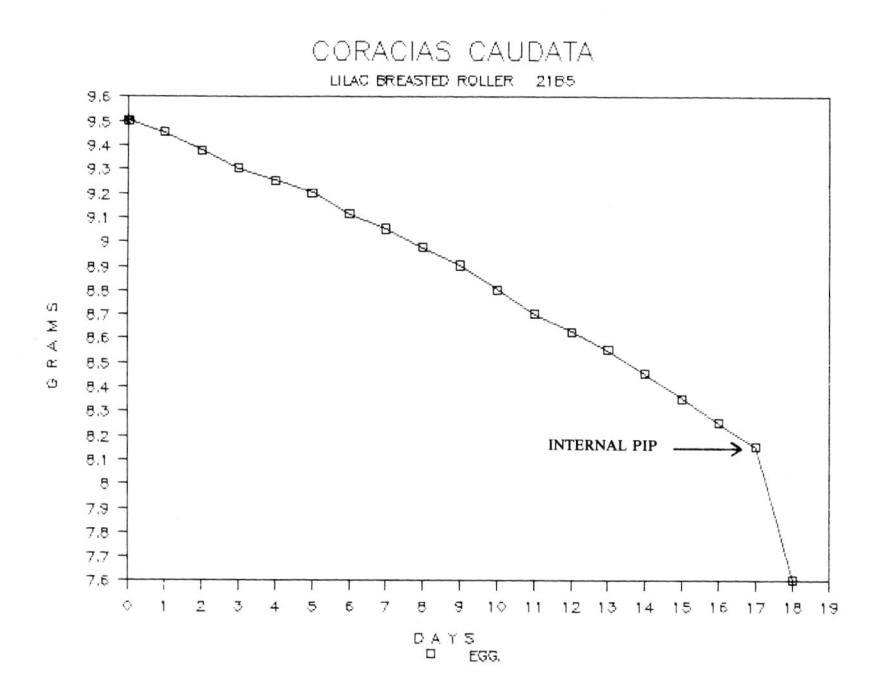

Fig 3.2; This graph shows the daily weight loss against the days of incubation for a Lilac brested roller egg.

PRACTICAL INCUBATION

down the moisture loss from the egg. Similarly, if an egg is not losing enough weight then it needs to be subjected to drier conditions in the incubator.

ARA ARARAUNA
BLUE & GOLD MACAW.

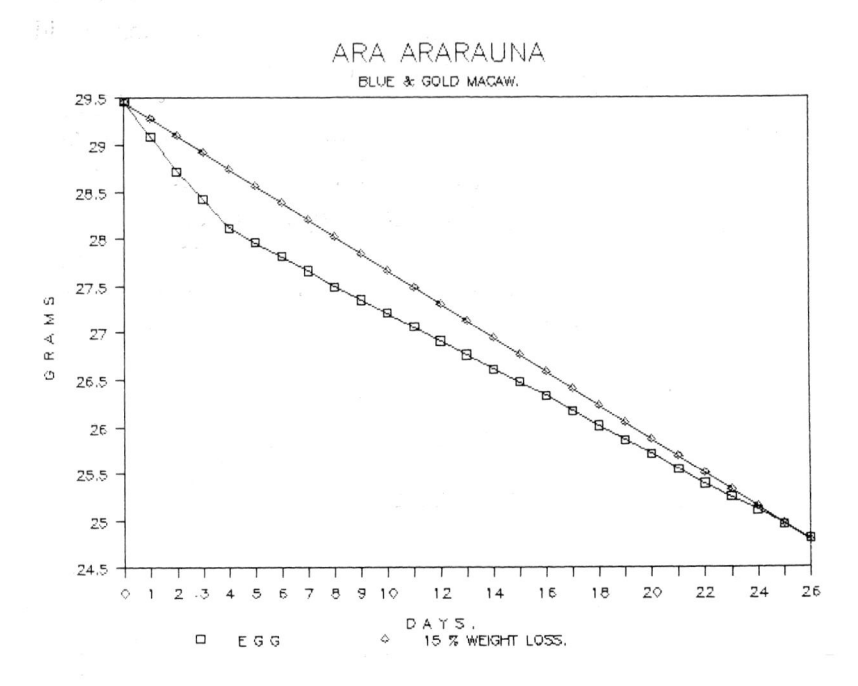

□ EGG   ◇ 15 % WEIGHT LOSS.

Fig 3.3; This graph shows the daily weight loss of a "porous" Blue and gold macaw egg against the days of incubation where the egg was moved to an incubator with high humidity on day 4.

This graph, Fig.3.3, shows a Blue and Gold Macaw (*Ara ararauna*) egg which, after 4 days of incubation, was heading towards a weight loss of nearly 30%. On day 4 the egg was moved from an incubator with a wet bulb reading of 83°F to an incubator where the wet bulb was 93°F. The higher the wet bulb reading the higher the humidity. This corrected the weight loss to approximately 15% at internal pip. If the egg had not been moved to an incubator with a higher humidity the chances of it hatching would have been very low indeed.

Of course the opposite can happen when an egg, after a few days of incubation, is heading towards a very low weight loss. This can be rectified by moving the egg to an incubator with a lower humidity, ie; a lower wet bulb reading.

MONITORING YOUR EGGS

This graph, Fig.3.4, shows an egg from a Humboldt Penguin (Spheniscus humboldti) was heading towards a weight loss of approximately 11.5% so on day seven it was moved to an incubator which had a very low humidity.

It is very difficult to change the weight loss of an egg after a third of t e incubation period has passed. By then it is as if the egg has made up its own mind. You can alter the weight loss by drastic means such as adding nail varnish to slow down weight loss or making a hole into the air space to increase weight loss. You will see on some of my graphs that I have changed the weight loss of eggs after this period but I have an incubation room where I can control the humidity very precisely. For most people this would not be possible.

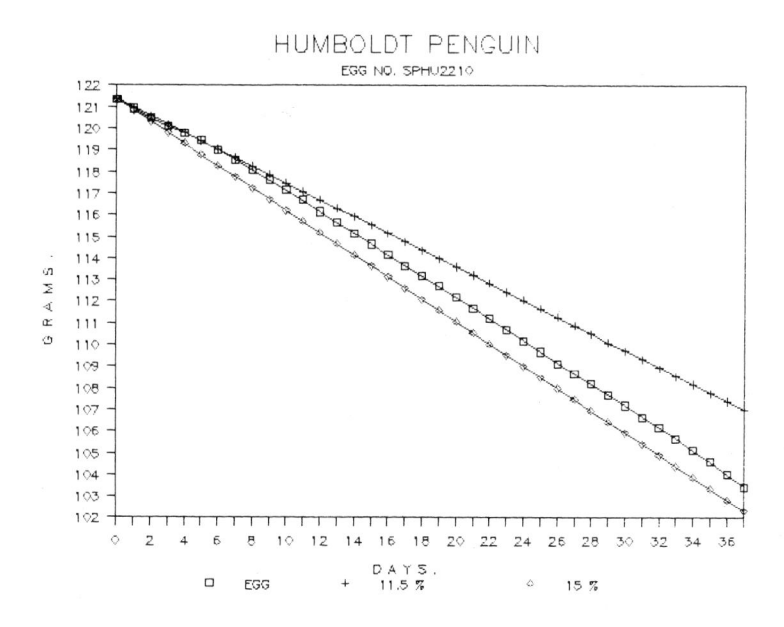

Fig 3.4; This graph shows the weight loss of a penguin egg against the days of incubation. The two straight lines are guide lines of 11.5 and 15% weight loss.

By far the simplest and safest way is to monitor the weight loss very accurately and move the egg after 3 or 4 days to an appropriate incubator.

PRACTICAL INCUBATION

Sometimes an egg might be moved 2 or 3 times during incubation to keep it at the correct weight loss.

GROUND HORNBILL.
EGG No. BUAB185.

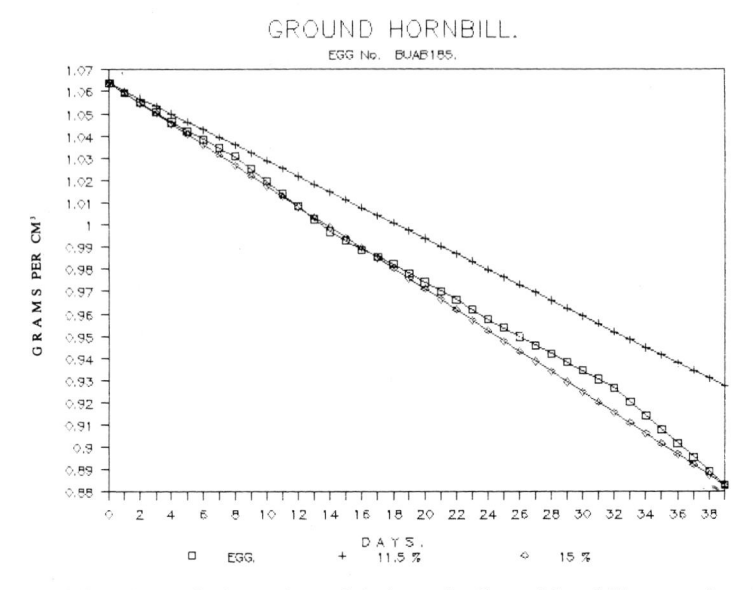

Fig 3.5; This graph shows the weight loss of a Ground hornbill egg against the days of incubation and demonstates how the weight loss can be controlled by moving the egg into incubators which are set with different wet bulb readings.

This graph, Fig.3.5., shows a Ground Hornbill egg (Bucorvis abyssinicus) that started in an incubator with wet bulb reading of 80°F. By day 8 you can see that the egg was heading towards a weight loss of approximately 12% so the egg was moved to an incubator where the wet bulb reading was 70°F By day 14 you can see the weight loss dipping below the 15% line so the egg was moved back to 80°F on the wet bulb. A final adjustment was made on day 31 when the egg was moved to 70°F again. You do not need to be as precise in controlling weight loss as shown on this graph but it is a good example of what can be achieved.

At this stage I must point out that weight loss techinques can improve your hatching results by as much as 10% or more. But it is a

MONITORING YOUR EGGS

complete waste of time using weight loss techinques if you are not cleaning and sterilising your eggs. Hatching success is greatly improved by being as hygienic as possible, handling eggs carefully and candling regularly. Weight loss techinques are the icing on the cake.

If you have several eggs from one clutch and the first few needed humidity X, do not presume the rest of the clutch will need the same. A good example of this was when I had a Vulturine Guinea Fowl lay thirteen fertile eggs. The first ten were in an incubator with a wet bulb reading of 84°F and they were all heading for a 15 % weight loss. The last three eggs were started in the same incubator but excessive weight loss was observed in only a couple of days. These eggs were then placed in an incubator with a wet bulb reading of 93°F. All thirteen eggs hatched successfully.

The last three eggs turned out to be thin shelled but of course when you pick an egg up it is very difficult to know whether it is thin shelled or not. A thin shelled egg normally means that the shell is very porous and therefore loses a lot of moisture in an incubator. Of course this is easily rectified by placing it in an incubator which is set at a very high humidity.

This is a straight forward example of the use of weight loss techniques to improve your results. However be warned that controlling weight loss in an egg is not always that easy. For example with african spoonbills (Platalea alba), most of their eggs if you take them as they are laid and place them in a very dry incubator lose hardly any weight.

The following graph, Fig.3.6, shows a typical example of the weight loss of an African Spoonbill egg, the cuticle of which was not removed.

The egg did not hatch!

When the African Spoonbill egg is dipped in sterilising solution it becomes very slippery. This is because it has a very thick cuticle. To hatch these eggs I found the best method was to gently scrub the thick slippery cuticle from the eggs before incubation commences. The eggs then behaved perfectly normally and it was easy to adjust their weight loss. When the adult birds sit on their eggs the thick cuticle is slowly removed as the eggs rub against the twigs that they

MONITORING YOUR EGGS

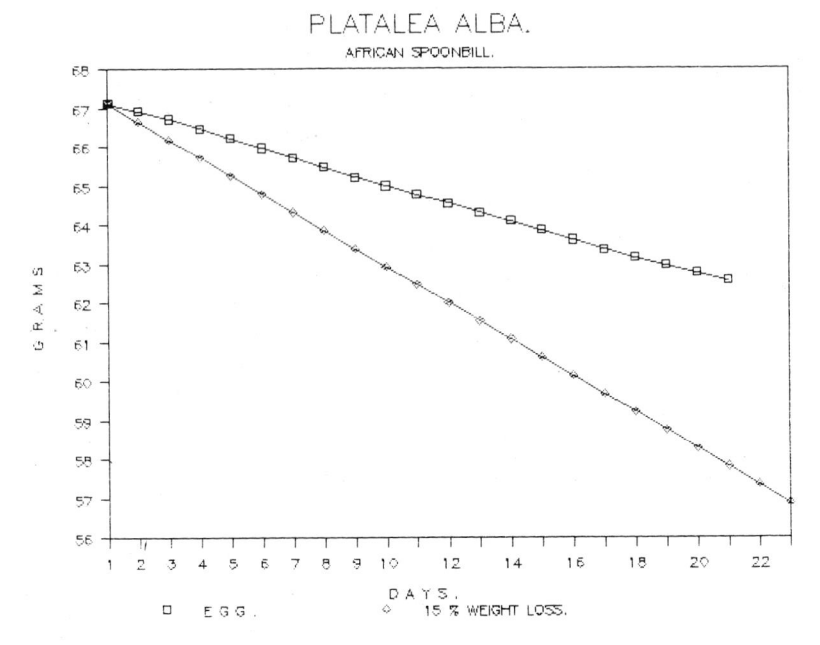

Fig 3.6; This graph shows the weight loss of a typical African spoonbill egg against the days of incubation when the cuticle has not been removed.

are resting on.

Of course the opposite sometimes happens. One good example where it was very difficult to stop an egg from losing too much weight was an Eclectus parrot egg (Eclectus roratus), Fig.3.7.

This particular egg after only two days of incubation had lost a massive amount of weight. It was then placed in an incubator at maximum humidity. Unfortunately this was not enough, so on day six nail varnish was added to slow down the weight loss.

As you can see the nail varnish which was added on day 6 had great effect. One more adjustment was made on day 22 when the egg was put in a slightly lower humidity.

The following graph, Fig.3.7, is a good example to showing how the weight loss was changed by drastic means to get it back to the 15 % that was desired. The egg did not hatch but ended up dead in shell. This was probably due to such massive weight loss in the early

MONITORING YOUR EGGS

stages of development so this is also an example of the sort of weight loss an egg cannot cope with.

The next egg from this pair of birds had the same very porous shell but this time nail varnish was added on day 2 and the egg was successfully hatched.

One other tip when monitoring weight loss is that if all the eggs from one incubator seem to be losing too much weight then check your wet bulb wick because it has probably slipped slightly off the thermometer or is soiled and giving a false reading ie it is reading higher than the true reading and therefore you think the incubator is more humid than it really is!

What you are trying to do is to build up a library of successful hatches for each species of bird eggs that you incubate. Then the following year you will know exactly what to expect from each species

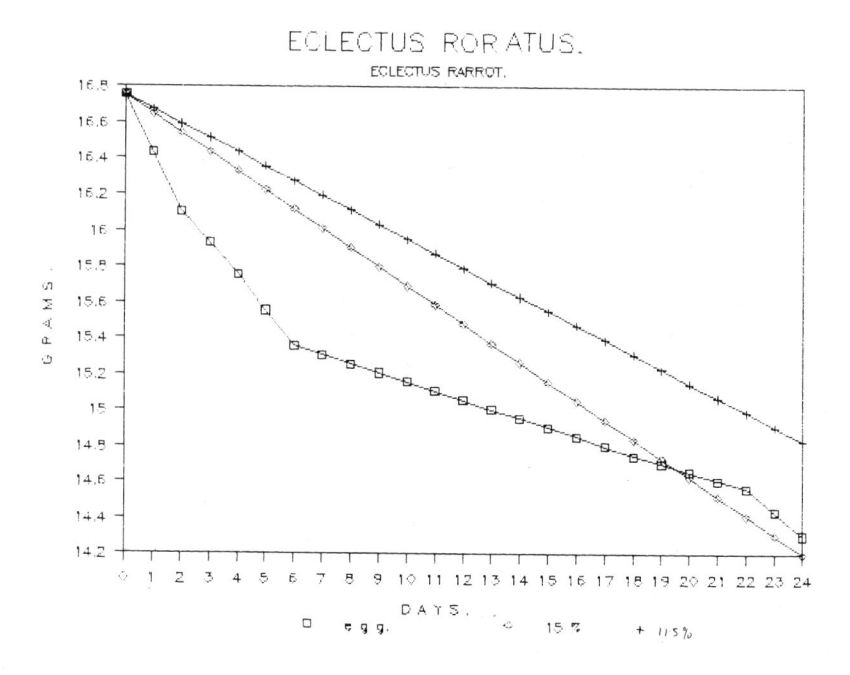

Fig 3.7; This graph shows the weight loss of a very porous Eclectus parrot egg against the days of incubation and how drastic measures are required in such cases to stop to much weight being lost.

MONITORING YOUR EGG

STONE CURLEW
WEIGHT LOSS

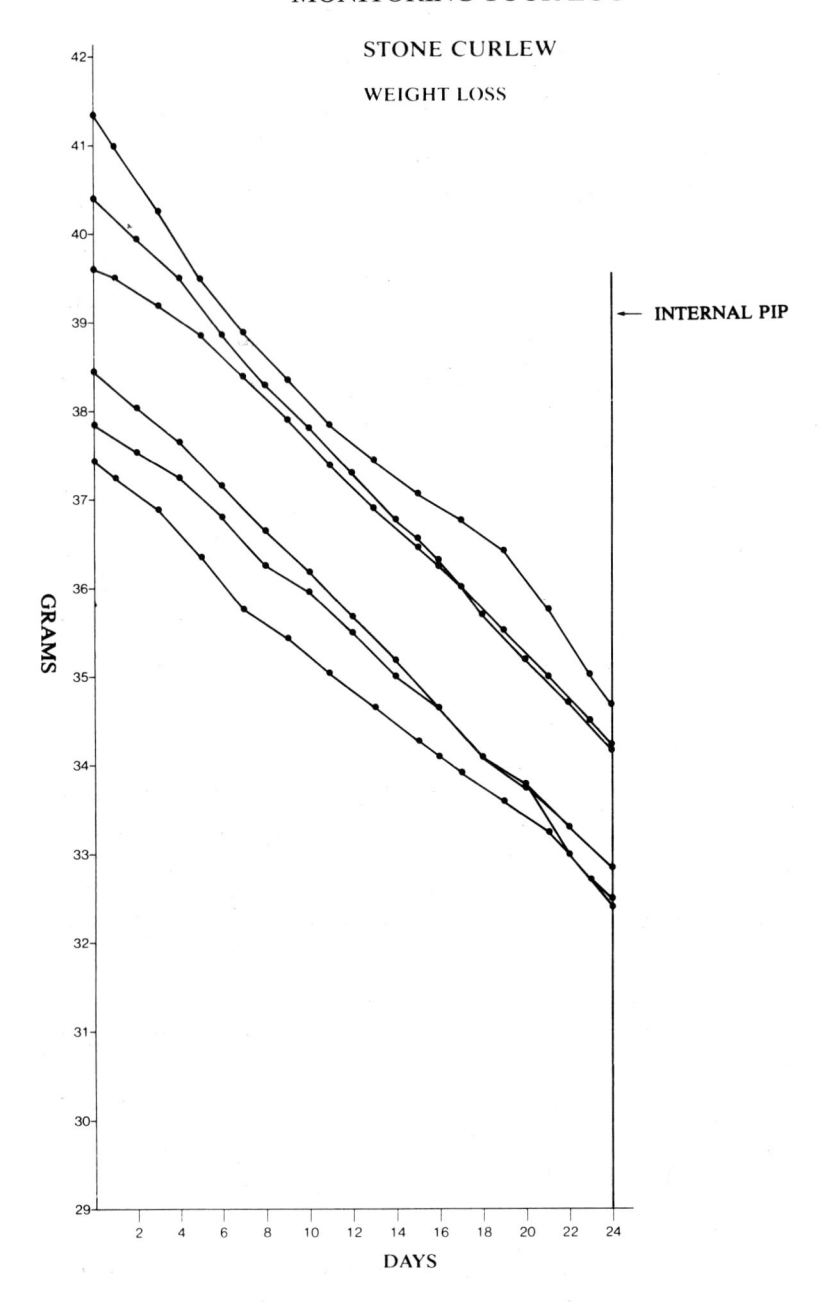

Fig 3.8; This graph shows the weight loss of 6 Stone curlew eggs against the days of incubation

MONITORING YOUR EGGS

I would strongly suggest you keep egg weight loss records for each pair of birds because although one particular species normally requires X reading on the wet bulb you will find that we all have at least one or two pairs of birds which lays odd eggs!

Use your records as a guide line only for the following year because strange things can happen. I had a pair of Roul Roul Partridges from which 25 young were reared in one year. All the eggs were artificially incubated at 99.5°F on the dry bulb and 83°F on the wet bulb.

The following year all the eggs that were laid needed to be in 93°F on the wet bulb to stop them losing too much weight! The interesting thing was that the first year the adult birds were in a very dry area on sand and the following year when the eggs needed higher humidity to hatch the adult birds were in a very humid tropical house.

I do not know if the adult birds can change the egg structure depending on the conditions where they live or whether they were just eating something different but it shows that all eggs need monitoring for maximum results.

3.C Density loss techniques

"DENSITY" is that word that we all used to know the meaning of when we were at school but now we are adults we have forgotten completely.

So what is density? The easiest way to explain is as follows

If you take a freshly laid egg and put it in a bucket of water, it sinks. The density of the egg is greater than 1.

If you take an egg that is near the end of its incubation period and place that in a bucket of water it will float. The density of this egg is less than 1.

At some point during the incubation period you will be able to place an egg into a bucket of water and it will neither float nor sink but just sit there. This egg has a density of 1.

Taking it one stage further,

Weight divided by volume = Density.

So if you have an object which weighs 1 gram and has a volume of 1 cubic cm then its density is 1 Divided by 1 = 1.

Sounds easy so far but we have a slight problem. Measuring the volume of a rectangular object is easy, it is length times breadth times depth, but an egg .... ?

We could measure the volume of an egg by placing it in a container of water which has markings on the side so we can just measure the amount of displaced water. I would not fancy doing this for every egg I have to incubate!

A more straight forward way to find the volume of an egg is by using a bit of simple mathematics.

The calculation we use is this:-

length x breadth x breadth x 0.51 = volume of an egg,

or LxBxBxO.51 = volume.

Of course eggs do vary slightly in shape so how can we have a figure of 0.51 for all eggs? Well I have tested many eggs from different species and the correction factor of 0.51 only varies by about 0.04 at the most. I believe that to work out the correction factor for every single species is not necessary, as 0.51 is very close for all species and in any case if the correction factor is 0.04 out, it will make hardly any difference on a density graph.

The easiest way to measure an egg is to use vernier callipers. With practice you will find them easy to use. There are now plastic vernier callipers available which are much cheaper than the normal metal ones.

The following is a typical example, (Table.3.1 page 58), of how we would monitor the density loss of an egg.

This egg was from a pair of Roul Roul partridges. You can see that three measurements were taken : the weight (g), length and breadth (cm). To calculate the volume we use LxBxBxO.51, i.e.

3.619 x 3.234 x 3.234 x 0.51 = 19.304 cm3

So the weight divided by the volume gives us a density of 1.046.

The calculation to find the volume is only done when you first get the egg. After this you simply weigh the egg every day or every other day and divide the weight by the volume.

The figure we are interested in is the average daily density loss. For example the average daily density loss for Roul Roul partridges is 0.010. The figure varies with different species.

If you have too high a density loss then you move the egg to an

MONITORING YOUR EGGS

incubator with a higher humidity to slow down the density loss. This is the same idea as the weight loss technique but it does have distinct advantages. You cannot give an average daily weight loss figure for eggs from one species as they vary in size. A large egg will lose more weight per day than a small egg from that species. How ever you can arrive at an average daily density loss because in so doing you are taking the size of the egg into account.

Once you have mastered density loss techniques it is not essentialto use graphs but they are nevertheless very informative. The following graphs, Figs.3.9 and 3.10 (pages 61,62), show ten Roul Roul partridge eggs. On one graph weight loss is shown and on the other density loss. These graphs show two advantages of density loss techniques.

Firstly you will notice that the lines are very close together on the density graph compared to the weight loss graph. Imagine you have picked up a Roul Roul partridge egg that has been incubated for an unknown period. You weigh the egg and it weighs 20 grams. By looking at the weight loss graph the egg could have just been laid or is just about to hatch! But if you then work out the density of the egg and it is for example, 0. 90 then you then work out the egg is between 12 and 14 days old. Some species of eggs are almost impossible to candle so this can be a very useful tool indeed.

Secondly you will notice that nearly all the eggs start between 1.03 to 1.05 on the density graph. The most dense part of an egg is the egg shell itself. If you get a freshly laid egg that has a very high start density compared to your past records (for example if you got a Roul Roul partridge egg that had a start density of 1.08) then you would have a good idea that that particular egg has a thick shell and will probably need an incubator with a lower humidity than you would normally use. The opposite applies when you get an egg with a low start density for that species. You will have a good idea that it is thinshelled and might need a higher humidity than normal to stop it losing too much weight/density.

So with density techniques you may be able to predict what humidity an egg will need during incubation before you start.

As a general rule a thin-shelled egg will need higher humidity during incubation to stop it losing too much weight where as a thickshelled egg will need a lower humidity during incubation to make it lose enough weight.

PRACTICAL INCUBATION

SPECIES	ROUL ROUL	DAY	WEIGHT	DENSITY	DAY LOSS	TEMP	WET BULB
PEN	LS 18	0	20.2	1.046		37.2°C	83°F
EGG NUMBER	J	1					
DATE	28/5	2	19.8	1.025	0.0105		
INC PERIOD	19	3					
INC TO I.P.	18	4	19.4	1.005	0.010		
WEIGHT	20.2	5					
LENGTH	3.619	6	19.05	0.986	0.0(95		
BREADTH	3.234	7					
VOLUME	19.304	8	18.65	0.966	0.010		
		9					
RESULTS		10	18.3	0.948	0.009		
		11					
GOOD HATCH		12	17.9	0.927	0.0105		
		13					
SHELL 0. 14mm		14	17.5	0.906	0.0105		
		15					
		16	17.05	0.883	0.0115		
INTERNAL PIP		17					
		18	16.7	0.865	0.009		
HATCHED		19					

Table 3.1; A simple way of writing down the results from monitoring eggs using density loss, this example was from a Roul roul partridge egg.

The following graphs, Figs.3.11 and 3.12, compare weight loss and density loss for Vulturine Guinea Fowl.

If you have only one egg on a graph it is possible to show both the weight and the density of an egg during incubation as seen on Fig.3.13, of an egg from a pair of Wandering Tree Pies.

The following graphs, Figs.3.14 and 3.15, are good examples of species of birds that normally have high start densities because they have thick shells.

All the eggs that I incubate are plotted on a graph that shows both density and weight loss. Basically it is a density graph but it has 11.5% and 15% weight loss lines on it. This is simply done by subtracting 15 % from the start weight, this being the weight that you are trying to reach at internal pip. By dividing this figure by the volume you have the density you want to achieve at internal pip. This figure is then put on the graph at the internal pip day and a line drawn from here to the density on day 0.

The same is then done for 11.5% weight loss.

MONITORING YOUR EGGS

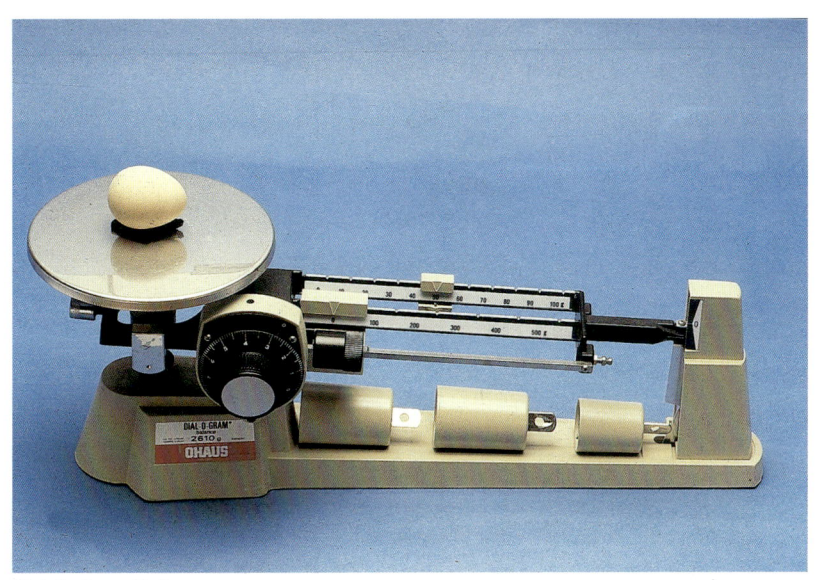

Triple Bean Balance

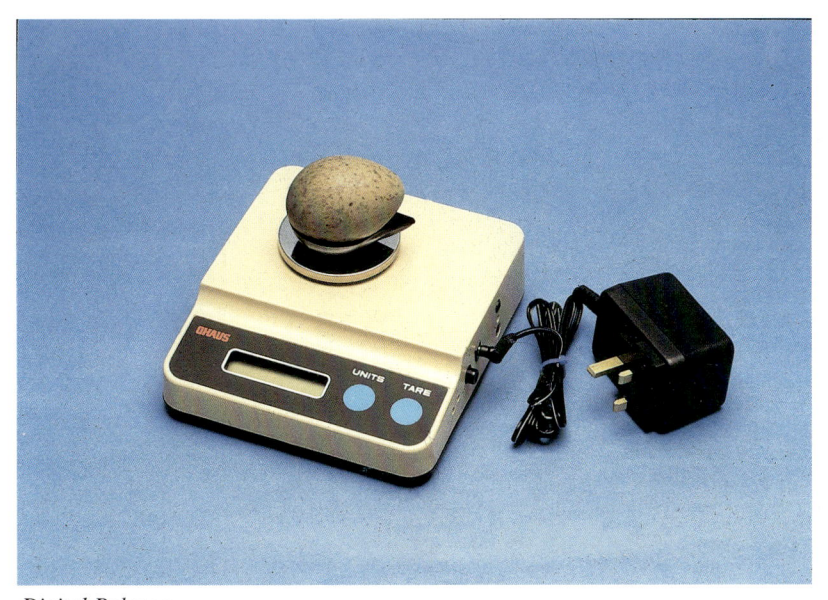

Digital Balance

PRACTICAL INCUBATION

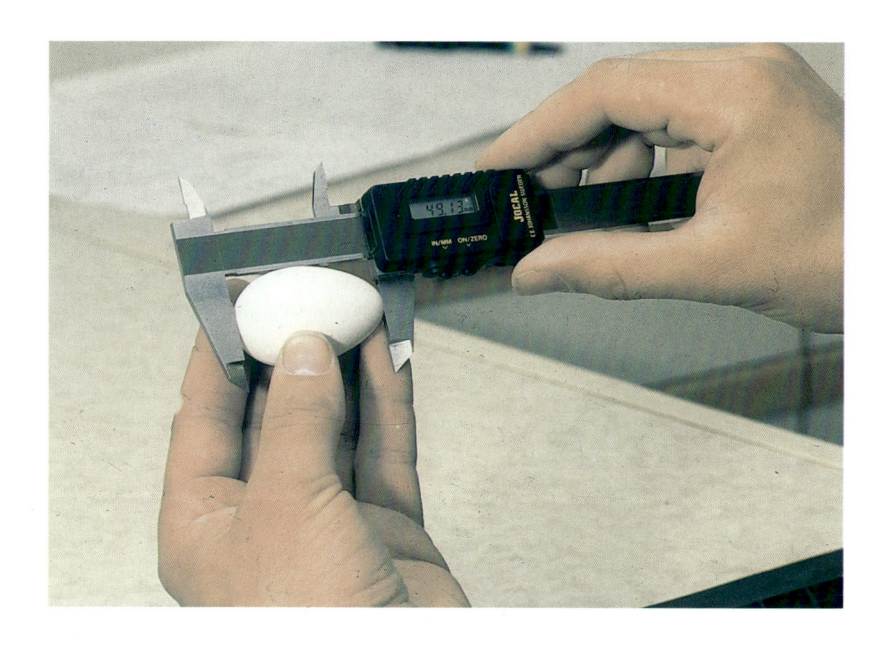

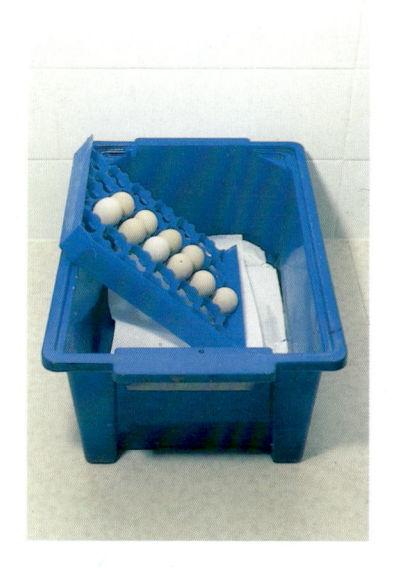

Above: Measuring an egg

Left: Storing eggs at an angle of 45 degrees

MONITORING YOUR EGGS

ROUL ROUL PARTRIDGE

WEIGHT LOSS

← INTERNALLY PIPPED

ALL GOOD HATCHES
TEMP 37.2°C
WET BULB 83°F
ALL HATCHED DAY 19.

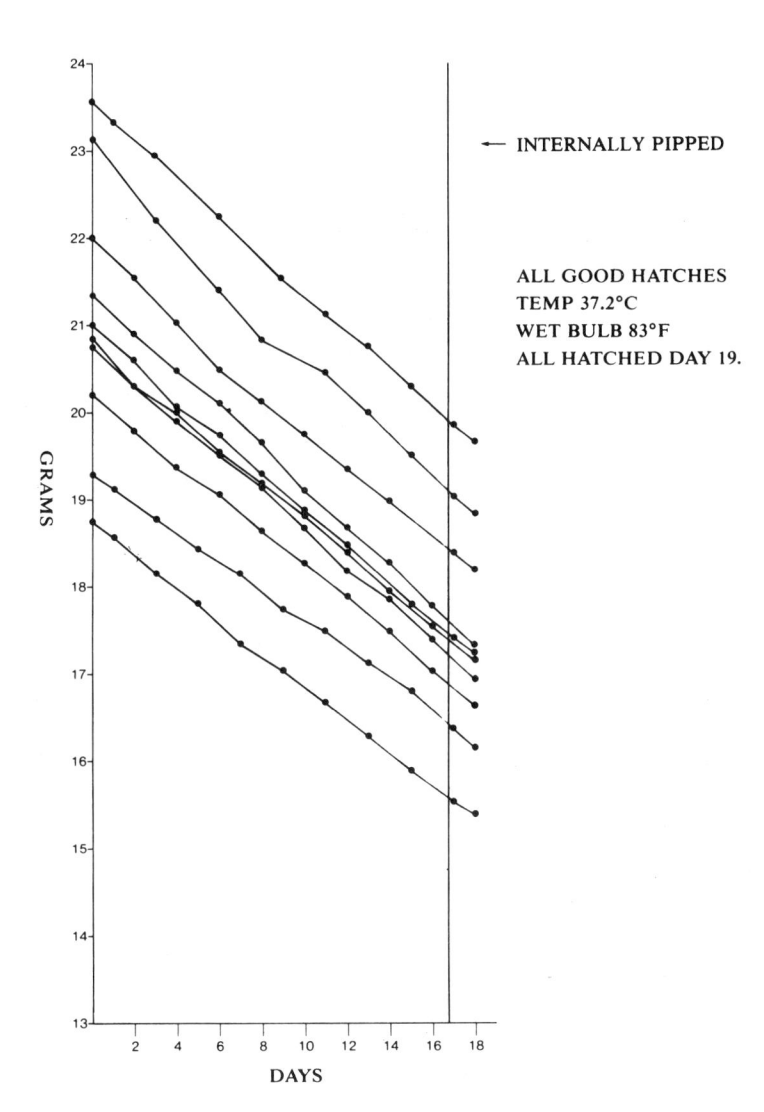

Fig 3.9; This graph shows the weight loss of 10 Roul partridge against the days of incubation

MONITORING YOUR EGGS

ROUL ROUL PARTRIDGE

AVERAGE DAILY DENSITY LOSS .010
ALL GOOD HATCHES
TEMP 37.2°C 99°F
TEMP WET BULB NORMALLY 83°F

← INTERNALLY PIPPED.

ALL HATCHED ON DAY 19.

Fig 3.10; This graph shows the density loss from 10 Roul partridge against the days of incubation

MONITORING YOUR EGGS

Whether you are using Density loss techniques or the more commonly used Weight loss techniques, you will need to start your eggs off in a particular humidity.

If you have kept good records from last year then you will not have a problem. In fact if you have kept records for each egg then you will know if any particular pair of birds throw odd eggs that need a strange humidity.

If you are not sure what humidity to use I suggest you start at 5 5 % Relative Humidity. On a wet bulb this would be 84.F presuming that you are incubating at 99.5F dry bulb.

If you are incubating large numbers of common pheasant or partridge eggs then this sort of humidity level will be fine until they start to pip when maximum humidity will be required.

For converting fahrenheit to centigrade see page 115. To work out your relative humidity see page 117.

The following are some guidelines for specific species but please remember these are averages and individual eggs can vary terrifically.

Species	WB.	RH.	Species	WB.	RH,
Pheasants	84.°F	55%	Spoonbills	70.°F	24%
Partridge	84.°F	55%	Guineafowl	84.°F	55%
Parrots	80-84.°F	45%-55%	Cranes	84.°F	55%
Waterfowl	84.°F	55%	Rollers	78.°F	42%
Penguins	75.°F	34%	Kookaburras	80.°F	45%
Ostrich	70.°F	24%	Oystercatcher	80.°F	45%
Rhea	80.°F	45%	Touraco	84.°F	55%

PRACTICAL INCUBATION

VULTURINE GUINEA FOWL

WEIGHT LOSS GRAPHS

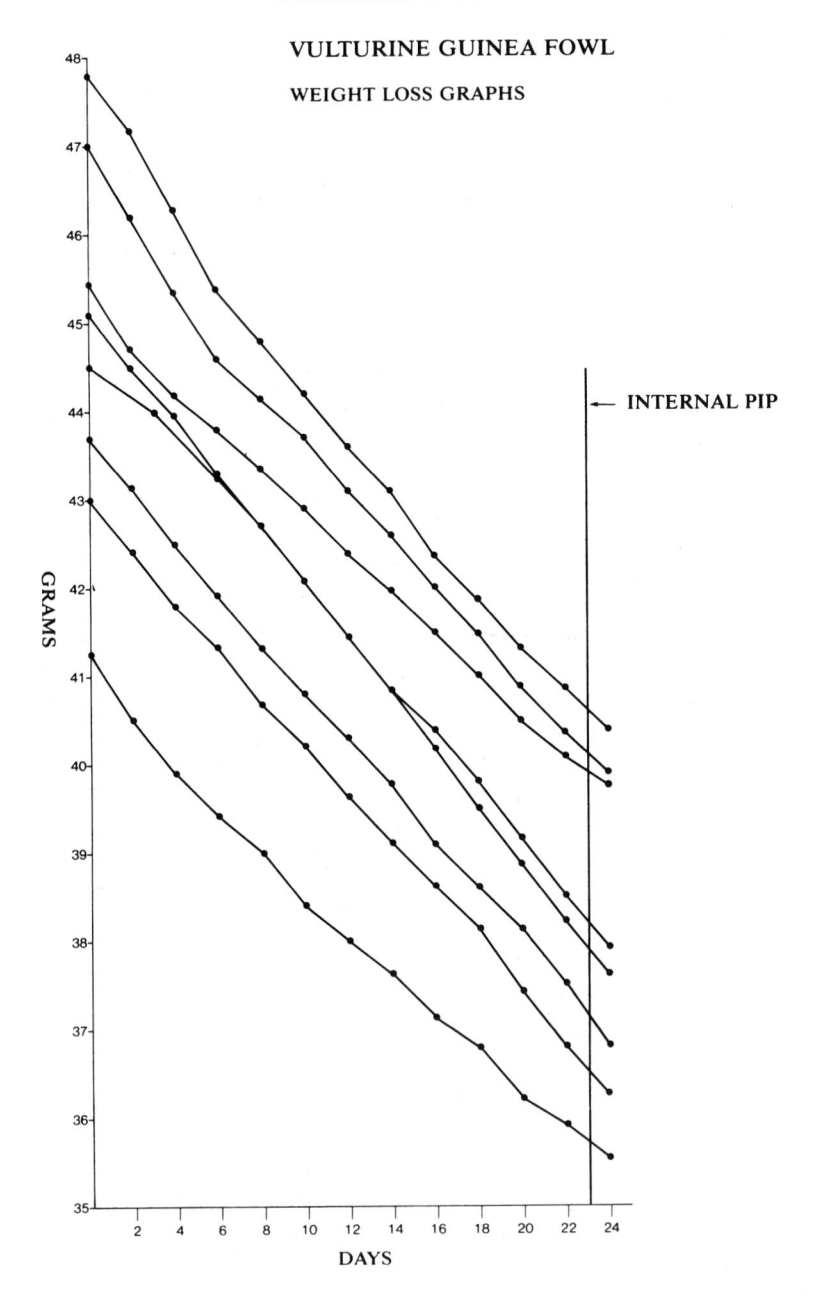

← INTERNAL PIP

Fig 3.11; This graph shows the weight loss of several Vulturine guinea fowl eggs against the days of incubation

MONITORING YOUR EGGS

VULTURINE GUINEA FOWL

AVERAGE DAILY DENSITY LOSS .0065
ALL GOOD HATCHES.   TEMP 37.2°C   99°F
TEMP WET BULB   NORMALLY 83°F

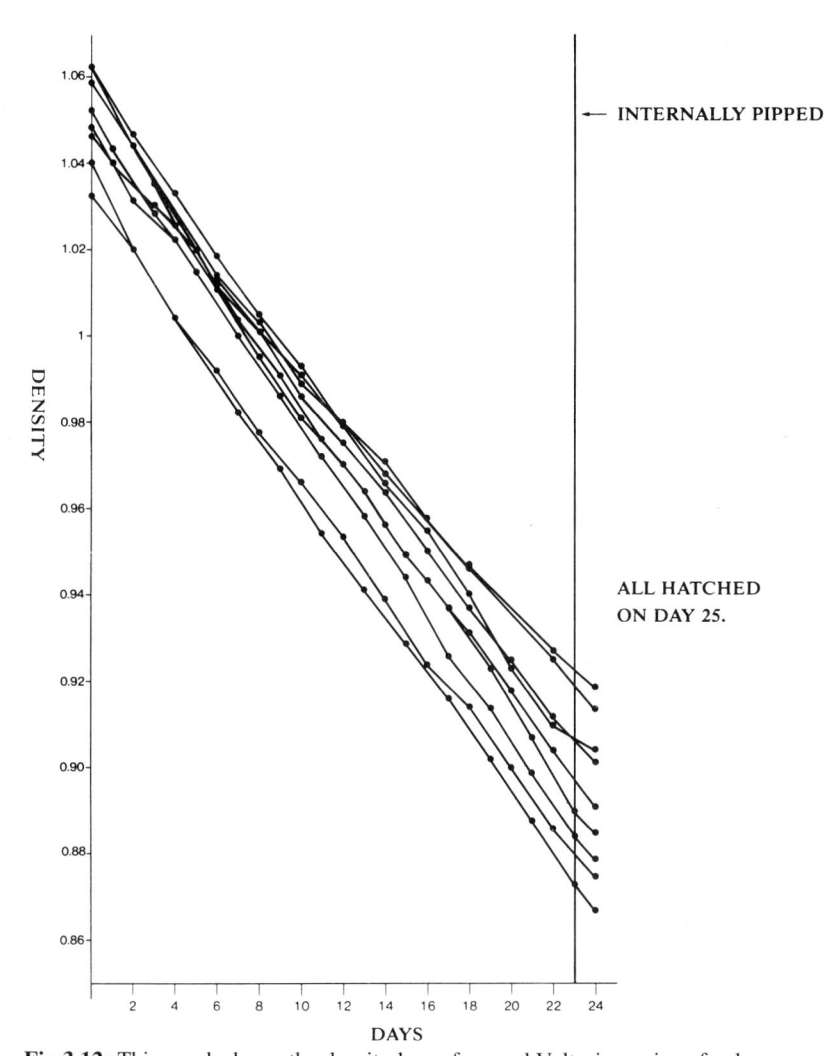

Fig 3.12; This graph shows the density loss of several Vulturine guinea fowl eggs against the days of incubation

PRACTICAL INCUBATION

WANDERING TREE PIE

EGG No.	WT. LOSS %	SHELL THICKNESS mm	INC TEMP °F	HUMIDITY °F
10A8	17.0	0.12	99.5	84

TURNING: BY HAND 7 ×/ DAY
+ MACHINE TURNING

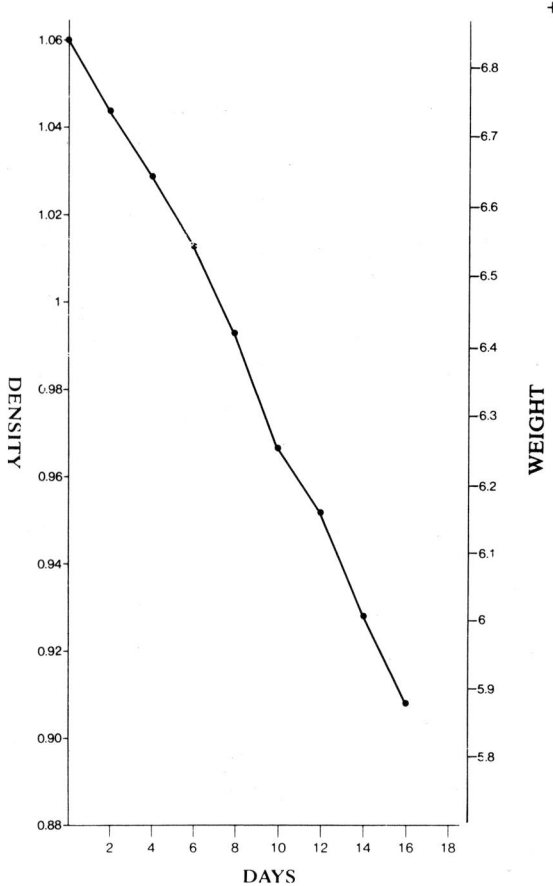

Fig 3.13; This graph shows the weight and density loss for a wandering treepie egg against the days of incubation.

MONITORING YOUR EGGS

OSTRICH

EGG No.	WEIGHT LOSS	SHELL THICKNESS	TEMP.	HUMIDITY
286	17.3%	2.01 mm	36.2 °C	OFF
246	19.6%	1.8 mm	36.2 °C	OFF
236	17%	1.82 mm	36.2 °C	OFF

TURNING: BY HAND SEVEN TIMES A DAY.

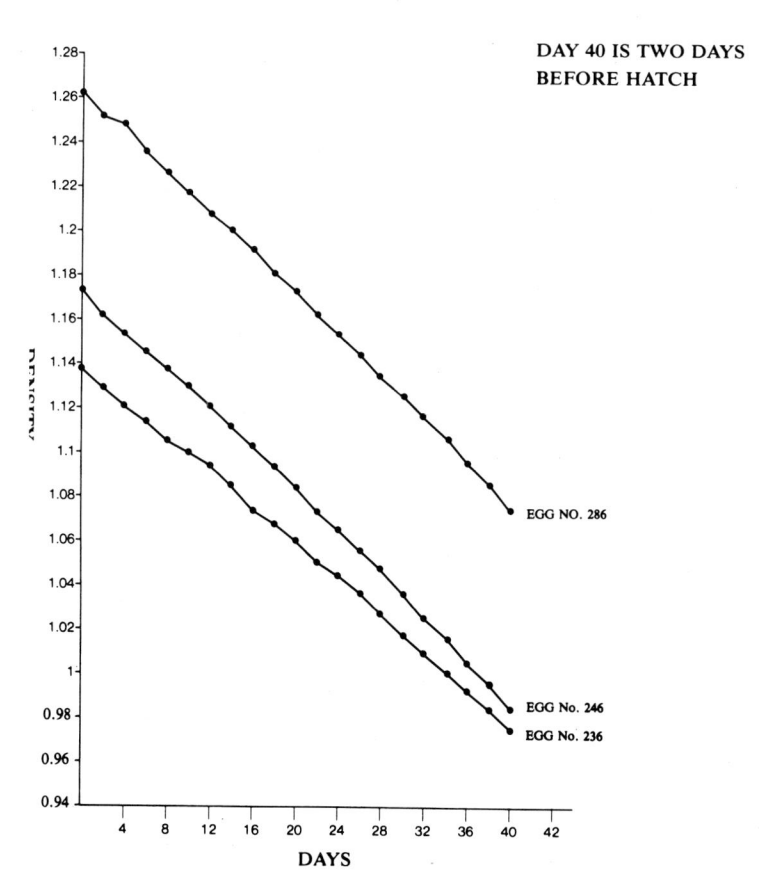

DAY 40 IS TWO DAYS BEFORE HATCH

Fig 3.14; This graph shows the Density loss of three ostrich eggs against the days of incubation.

PRACTICAL INCUBATION

COMMON GUINEA FOWL

AVERAGE DAILY DENSITY LOSS 0.005
ALL GOOD HATCHES
TEMP 37.2°C 99°F
TEMP WET BULB NORMALLY 83°F

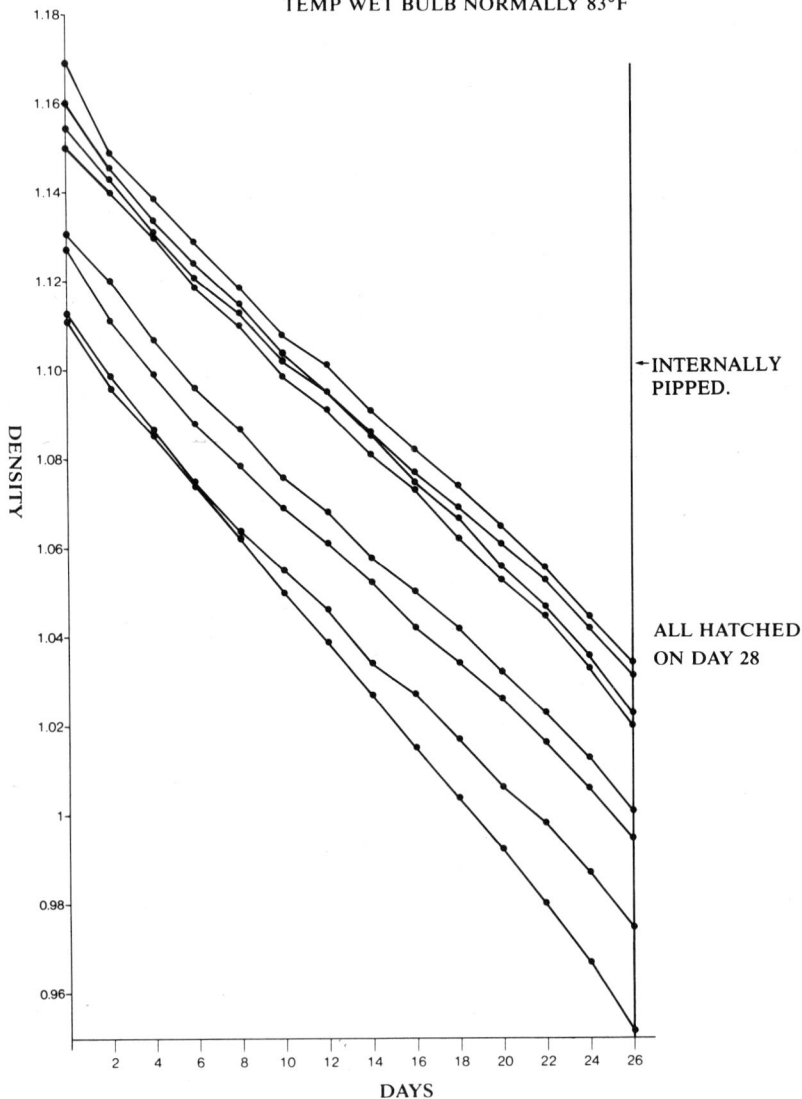

← INTERNALLY PIPPED.

ALL HATCHED ON DAY 28

Fig 3.15; This graph shows the density loss from several Common quinea fowl eggs against the days of incubation.

MONITORING YOUR EGGS

The following, Fig.3.16, is a typical graph that I would use, a density graph but with 15% weight loss lines drawn on it.

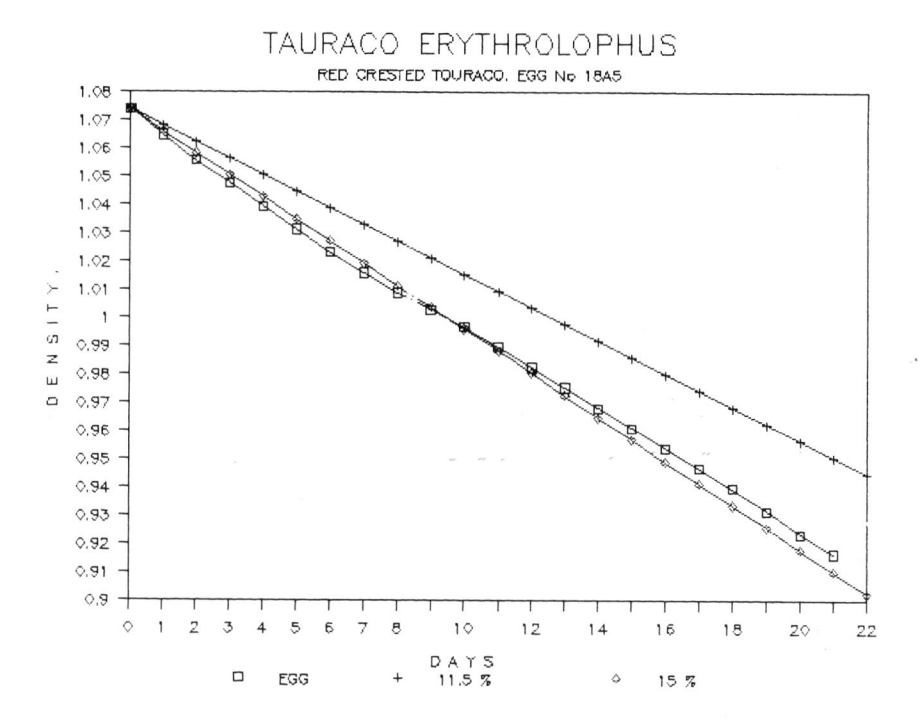

Fig 3.16; This graph of the density loss of a Red crested touraco against the days of incubation is typical of what the computer would display on screen

4 Other Considerations

4.A Storing eggs

Storing eggs can be a good idea in some circumstances.

If you rear pheasants for example, it is much easier to have several chicks hatch at the same time so that they can be reared together. On the other hand birds such as parrots are normally reared individually in which case storing the eggs is not necessary.

Most eggs can be stored for seven days without any problems. As a guide line, the larger the egg the longer it can be stored. Fertile eggs do die if stored for too long. But, for example, if a hundred fertile bantam eggs are stored for a week you may only lose one egg. If they are stored for ten days you may lose three, two weeks you may lose ten and so on.

Sometimes it is better to risk losing a few eggs during storage if the young of that species are very difficult to rear individually. If for example you lose ten percent of your eggs by storing too long but the mortality rate of rearing the young individually is thirty percent, then storing the eggs is a good idea because the chicks will hatch together and can be reared together to give you a better return.

With parrots which are reared individually by hand, storing eggs should not be risked.

Obviously the longer the egg has to wait to go into an incubator the greater the risk of bacterial infection through the egg shell. Before you store your eggs clean off any muck and dip them in one of the many brands of egg disinfectant on the market. Also I would recommend dipping the eggs once more before you put them into the incubator.

The best way to store eggs is, firstly, in a temperature of approximately 55°F and secondly in a slightly humid atmosphere.

PRACTICAL INCUBATION

Cellars are good places in which to store eggs as the temperature does not vary much in a twenty four hour period.

Your eggs will need turning even though they are not being incubated because the yolk will slowly float to the top of the egg and this will be fatal. The eggs will require turning either once or three times a day, always an odd number so that they are on a different side each night. If you have a lot of eggs to turn you can put your eggs on an egg tray and tilt the tray 45° one way and then to turn them just tilt the tray 45° the other way.

I suggest you mark and date all your eggs before you store them because if you have a lot of eggs and a memory like mine, trying to remember which eggs came in several days ago can be difficult.

WARNING:

If eggs are stored in temperatures approaching 70°F they will slowly start to develop, become weak and die!!

4.B Bantams as incubators

Type of bantam:-
There are many types of bantam on the market and often you will hear people say " these are best or those are best " but I prefer a good Silky cross Bantam or sometimes a pure Silky. It is not of great importance - what is important is how each individual bird performs.

What type of eggs can they sit on ?

Any egg from a partridge, pheasant, duck, goose or crane. Obviously a large bantam is required for crane eggs and she can only sit on one or two of these large eggs. At the other end of the scale if you intend to incubate partridge eggs a smaller bantam is probably a better choice.

Size of the egg is not the only limitation. Parrot eggs of some species are larger than partridge eggs but too delicate for bantams to sit on. Also some eggs require very high or very low humidities and therefore it is better to use an incubator of the mechanical kind for them.

Housing:

Bantams can be kept outside in a wire pen, preferably with a wire roof to keep out other birds. If you do not have a wire roof to your

OTHER CONSIDERATIONS

pen then make sure there are not any trees or objects near to the perimeter wire of your pen because, although bantams are generally not good flyers, they will jump from branch to branch to escape or roost.

Some sort of shelter is needed in the outside pen, a lean-to shelter or preferably a small hutch. Of course, bantams can be kept completely inside as well, but wherever you keep your bantams, provide them with a clean enviroment. They may be only bantams but these birds are going to sit on your valuable eggs.

One other thing about your pen is that it should have a good light which can be put on in the evenings early in the year. Often you will have eggs to incubate before you have any broodies. By prolonging daylight hours you will get your bantams to go broody earlier.

Preparation before use:-

Before the season starts you must dust your bantams for flees and lice and worm them otherwise if you intend to use a broody bantam for hatching, she will pass on the parasites to the newly-hatched chicks. Dusting and worming powders can be obtained from your local vet. Check the toe nails in case they need clipping. I cannot stress enough that the better you look after your bantams, the healthier and better incubators they will be.

Next, place nesting sites for them to start laying their eggs in. Whether you use expensive ready-made laying boxes, or nail old apple boxes to the shed or shelter, is not important, as long as they are happy to lay in them.

It is a good idea to date the eggs that the bantams lay for two reasons. Firstly only about 8-12 eggs in one basket are necessary and if you mark them as they are laid then once you reach this number you can take the newly laid eggs knowing that they are freshly laid.

Secondly you need to stop unwanted chicks from hatching. As you take one broody away often another will take its place in the same basket so some eggs do get incubated for 21 days. Because you have dated them, they can be thrown away at two weeks old if necessary.

My memory is not that good from one year to another so just in case yours is not, I think it is of vital importance to ring all bantams so you know exactly which is which. And when one bird sits well or makes a good mother to newly-hatched chicks, then write this down

PRACTICAL INCUBATION

in your "Bantam Book" so next year you will know that your precious eggs will go under this bird and that bird will be used for rearing etc.

If a bird is broody for a few days then stops sitting or breaks eggs or you do not want to use her for whatever reason, get rid of her. Always keep many more bantams than you require and by disposing of bad birds over a few years you will end up with a good steady bunch of incubators.

Types of boxes for Broodies:

There are two main types of boxes:

Firstly a wooden box with a removable lid and a sliding door at the front leading to a small wire pen. The box should be slightly larger than your largest bantam so as to accommodate any of your birds. The inside has a wooden floor but the outside wire pen is open to the ground. This type of box can easily be moved daily and can be used for hatchlings if you wish. It should be kept on grass and moved every day after the bantam has been allowed to feed.

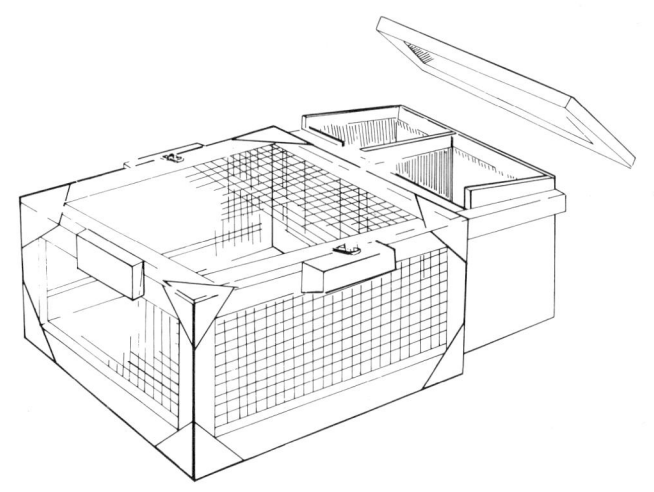

Diagram 4.1; A typical movable broody box.

OTHER CONSIDERATIONS

The second type is not unlike the first but it is not movable and is three feet off the ground. The idea is that it stands next to a shed or fence and the outside wire pen has wire on the floor. When the bantam is allowed to the outside pen any waste food or muck falls through the wire and can be cleaned up daily.

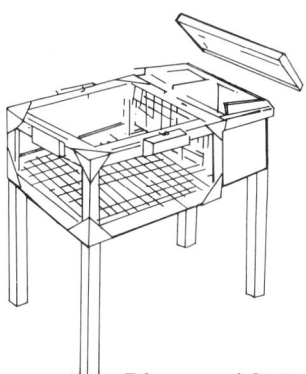

Diagram 4.2; A free standing broody box

Either hay or straw can be used for nests in the broody boxes, about three inches thick and packed down in the middle to make a nest. Before doing this put some dusting powder on the, floor of the box to help keep fleas at bay. If your boxes are of the movable type don't build them too heavy as they will need to be moved every day for hygienic reasons and to avoid killing off the grass.

If you want to apply wood preservative to your boxes do it at the end of the season because the lingering smell can put your broodies off from sitting.

To clean your boxes after use, scrape off any muck and scrub out with disinfectant. Soaking the box in water for twenty minutes before you start to clean them will help to remove any stubborn dirt.

The positioning of the boxes is important so as to avoid disturbance as far as possible - no dogs, noisy children, vermin or any other nuisance which might disturb your incubators.

OTHER CONSIDERATIONS

Feeding routines:

The broody need only be let out once a day but make sure it is the same time each day. If you are a few hours late she may start mucking in the box and fowling the eggs.

A good bird will eat, drink and excrete quickly and be back in the box before ten minutes is up. If the broody has not gone back in her box in ten minutes then carefully put her back. Each broody has her own character. Some broodies will always have to be put back in their box - this does not necessarily mean that they are bad broodies.

On the first day the broody is let out she may not come out so a little help is necessary. After a couple of days as soon as the door is opened she will be eager to come out.

After five days or so your broody is ready for your precious eggs. By this time you should know your bantam very well. Put your eggs under her when she is let out for her daily routine. Lock her out while you swap over the eggs because sometimes this can upset your broody if she can see you touching her nest. Remove the eggs that you have been using to find out if she is a good broody, remove the bedding and re-dust the floor. Put in fresh bedding making a nest out of it and put your new eggs in. If this is done during her 10 minute feed, drink and excrete routine she should not get disturbed at all and will happily accept her new eggs.

Good coding of all eggs is of vital importance. At the beginning of the season you will remember when you put the eggs under a particular broody but chaos soon reigns and so reliable codes are the only way. Writing on eggs is best done with a waterproof felt-tip pen as this will not get rubbed off under the broody.

The time to candle your eggs and remove any bad or infertile ones is again when she is in her feeding routine so there is no disturbance.

Do not put too many eggs under your broodies. Even one too many is disastrous because as she rotates the clutch of eggs each one will have its turn at being chilled and possibly killed.

If you are going to use the broody for hatching pour some water around the edge of the nest box when she is let out to be fed. This is to insure that the eggs will be in a humid environment which will make it easier for them to hatch.

Make sure all the eggs under her are due to hatch on the same day

OTHER CONSIDERATIONS

because once she thinks they have all hatched she will leave any odd ones. Once a broody has hatched a clutch of eggs it is inadvisable to introduce other hatchlings because she may not accept them. A trick that sometimes works is to lock her and her chicks into the broody box then add the new chicks as well. This way when you let her out the new chicks will have her smell and she will be more likely to accept them.

With more delicate chicks it might be a good idea to move the bantam and hatchlings indoors. This is always a good idea when dealing with crane chicks as a bantam would have problems keeping a chick this big warm.

4.C Using broodies and incubators together

This can be a very useful technique which is mainly used for grounddwelling birds. The idea is to incubate the eggs under broody bantams for the first 7 to 14 days and then transfer the eggs to an incubator.

The most important time when incubating your eggs is the first part of the incubation period. During the first ten days or so temperature, humidity and turning are all critical. If any of these are wrong during this period it could lead to the death of the developing chick, or weaken it so that it dies at the end of the incubation period just before it is due to hatch.

With this technique you are relying on the broody to incubate the eggs for the critical period before moving the eggs to an incubator. It can also save you some time because you do not have to monitor your eggs so closely in the early stages of incubation. However there are a few things you need to watch out for. Firstly, as the eggs are starting their life under a bantam they are much more likely to be attacked by bacteria. You will need to keep your incubators very clean because every now and again you may be placing an infected egg into an incubator. Remember an egg can be infected with bacteria and still be alive so it is possible that, even if you candle all your eggs when you take them from the broody to make sure they are alive, you may be putting the other eggs at risk!

PRACTICAL INCUBATION

The broody bantam is not a miracle worker. If an egg is placed under her that needs high humidity because it has a porous or thin shell she cannot compensate for the excessive weight loss and the egg will be lost.

Although most eggs will do fine, a small percentage of awkward eggs will be lost. To find out which eggs are suitable for a broody see page 72.

Movable broody bantam pens

4.D Hatching time

Just because you have managed to hatch an egg does not necessarily mean that the incubation conditions used were correct.
This statement is best explained by an example :-

Supposing you have ten fertile bantam eggs and incubate them at a temperature that is 2 degrees low or a humidity that is extremely high then you may hatch only one of these eggs because the incubation conditions were obviously wrong. If you hatch an egg from a species you have not incubated before, it might be that the egg that hatched was by chance the one in ten as with the bantam eggs.

We can get a good indication whether the incubation conditions were correct by examining the newly hatched chick. Also how the chick hatched can give us some clues.

So what does a normal chick look like?

Basically a normal chick is one that hatched on time and without any

OTHER CONSIDERATIONS

help, other than which it is very difficult to describe how they should look! Instead I will describe some of the common problems seen at hatch.

1.

If the chick seems to have difficulty in the final push out from the egg shell after it has broken the shell all round and if the chick then feels sticky, check the hatcher.

The most common cause of this problem is simply that the hatcher is not humid enough. The chick finds it difficult to rotate in the egg because it is drying out and becoming sticky. The chick must be able to rotate freely inside the egg in order to break the shell all round the blunt end of the egg.

If the humidity was too low during the whole incubation period then this will also cause this sort of problem at hatch.

2.

If after hatching the chick seems swollen or seems rather large for the egg, then perhaps the humidity during the incubation period has been too high and the chick has not lost enough water.

Remember that if the egg did not lose enough weight or it lost too much weight during incubation, it will still need maximum humidity once it has internally pipped to be able to hatch.

3.

If a chick hatches very early then it might simply be that the incubation temperature was too high. If you think you are incubating at the correct temperature then check your thermometer.

4.

If chicks are pipping and hatching, late then it could be that the incubation temperature was too low. Often you may have to give a bit of help to get the chick out of the egg shell in such cases.

Also if an egg gets temporarily chilled during incubation it might hatch 1 or 2 days late.

The four problems listed above are the most common but the following diagram, 4.3; is an easy-to-follow problem guide and gives some other reasons for specific problems at hatch and during incubation.

OTHER CONSIDERATIONS

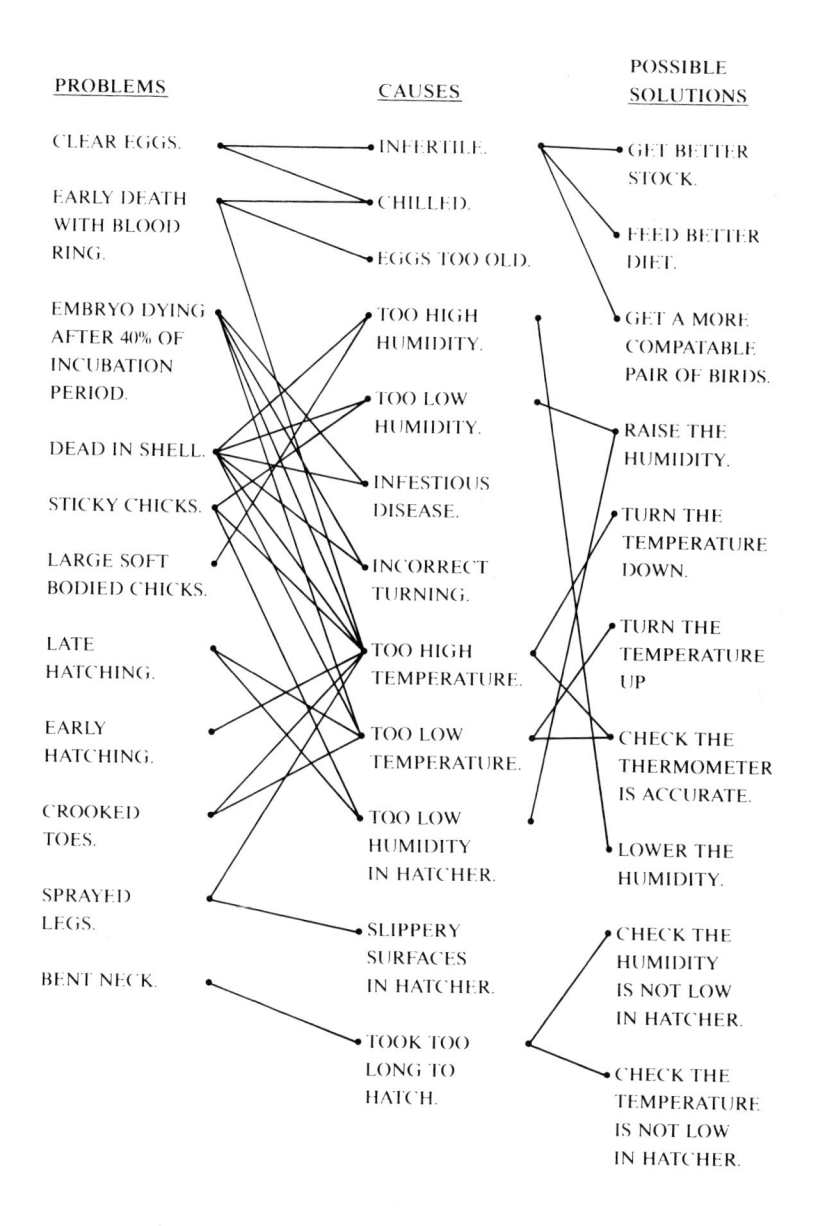

PROBLEMS	CAUSES	POSSIBLE SOLUTIONS
CLEAR EGGS.	INFERTILE.	GET BETTER STOCK.
EARLY DEATH WITH BLOOD RING.	CHILLED.	FEED BETTER DIET.
	EGGS TOO OLD.	
EMBRYO DYING AFTER 40% OF INCUBATION PERIOD.	TOO HIGH HUMIDITY.	GET A MORE COMPATABLE PAIR OF BIRDS.
	TOO LOW HUMIDITY.	RAISE THE HUMIDITY.
DEAD IN SHELL.	INFESTIOUS DISEASE.	TURN THE TEMPERATURE DOWN.
STICKY CHICKS.	INCORRECT TURNING.	
LARGE SOFT BODIED CHICKS.	TOO HIGH TEMPERATURE.	TURN THE TEMPERATURE UP
LATE HATCHING.	TOO LOW TEMPERATURE.	CHECK THE THERMOMETER IS ACCURATE.
EARLY HATCHING.	TOO LOW HUMIDITY IN HATCHER.	LOWER THE HUMIDITY.
CROOKED TOES.	SLIPPERY SURFACES IN HATCHER.	CHECK THE HUMIDITY IS NOT LOW IN HATCHER.
SPRAYED LEGS.	TOOK TOO LONG TO HATCH.	CHECK THE TEMPERATURE IS NOT LOW IN HATCHER.
BENT NECK.		

OTHER CONSIDERATIONS

4.E Detective work on failures

Why did it not hatch ? What did I do wrong ?

These are questions that we all ask ourselves every time an embryo dies during incubation or a chick dies just after hatching. And remember if a chick dies even a couple of weeks after it has hatched then the cause could have something to do with how it was incubated. This is where keeping very good results comes in.

The first piece of advice is do not jump to conclusions. You must look at everything very methodically before deciding " well it was probably this or that ". The reason I say this is because, if you do not look far enough, you may miss something and then correct something that does not need correcting

Clear eggs.

If an egg shows no sign of development after a week of being in an incubator then the chances are that it is not fertile.

On the other hand if a fertile egg gets badly chilled in the first couple of days then it will probably die and when you candle it you will see no sign of any growth because it is too small to see. The egg might not have been chilled in your incubator; it could be that the parent birds started to sit for a day or so and then left the nest site. If you discovered the egg the next day you might presume that it had just been laid.

This is a good example of why you must not jump to conclusions too quickly. If no development can be seen by day 7 then you know that the egg was probably infertile but you also need to check your incubator and watch your adult birds a bit closer when they are laying, just in case!

Early death.

If an egg dies after a few days of incubation, then by candling it you will see a clear egg except for a small blood ring. This is normally caused by either the incubation temperature being too high or the egg has been chilled.

If you are storing eggs and an egg gets stored for too long a period then this also can cause the early death of an egg.

PRACTICAL INCUBATION

Late death.

If an egg dies after approximately 40% of the incubation period has passed, then the two most likely causes for this are the wrong incubation temperature and possibly incorrect turning.

There are two other reasons why a developing chick can die at almost any time during incubation. The first reason which is very common is if bacteria have infected the embryo. This can cause death in the early stages of development or when the chick is about to hatch. It can also cause the death of a chick several days after it has hatched! If you send any fertile eggs that have died during incubation for a post mortem then you will know if this has happened.

The second reason is that if the adult stock is closely related then they will produce eggs that have weak embryos which tend to die about half way through the incubation period. Please look at every possibility first before you come to this conclusion because you may have missed something.

Dead in shell.

The most common problem is what is called " dead in shell

Dead in shell means that the chick started to breathe then died before it hatched. The chick does not need to have pipped in order to start breathing. The chick will start to breathe the air in the air space before breaking the egg shell.

Dead in shell can be caused by several things such as wrong temperature, wrong humidity, wrong turning and of course infectious disease.

So where do you start to look for the reasons why?

I would suggest using a process of elimination.

The first thing to do is to send the egg for a post mortem. If an infectious disease is discovered then you have the answer to why the chick died and you can start to look at your hygiene techniques during incubation or perhaps the nest site hygiene.

If the post mortem report shows no sign of an infectious disease then this is where good records start to help.

If you have kept daily records of the temperature of your incubator and there are no odd readings then you can rule out the

OTHER CONSIDERATIONS

wrong temperature. Of course this is assuming that you are using a temperature which is correct for that species of egg. If you know of someone successfully hatching this species at this temperature then you can be sure this is the right temperature to use. Most eggs require 37.5°C or 99.5°F Before you completely rule out temperature check that the thermometer is correct. See chapter on thermometers page 20.

If you have used weight or density loss techniques during incubation then you will have records for every egg, so if an egg ends up " dead in shell " you will know if the humidity was wrong during incubation. If you have not used weight loss techniques then the post mortem may suggest whether the weight loss was correct or not but you will probably have to ask them to look for this when submitting the egg.

If you have ruled out wrong temperature, wrong humidity and an infectious disease then look at turning. See the chapters on "candling" and "turning". If you have kept records of what you saw every time you candled your eggs then you will have a good idea if the turning was wrong.

If you can find no reason at all why the egg ended up " dead in shell " keep this in mind :

If the egg has come from badly fed parents or closely related parents then the egg could be considered as sub standard, so that although the embryo develops during incubation it is too weak to hatch.

Also if an egg was handled roughly during incubation it might have weakened the developing chick so again it is not strong enough to hatch.

I hope you can see from the above how important it is to keep records of everything you do in your incubation room and exactly how each egg was incubated. The following, Fig.4.1 and Table 4.1 is a typical example of the information I would have for each egg that I have incubated.

PRACTICAL INCUBATION

SPECIES CHARADR11FORMES BURHINIDAE *BURHINUS OEDICNEMUS*

PEN	SI	DAY 1	45S SIDE 3
EGG NO	45	DAY 3	FERTILE
DATE	4,5,89	DAY 5	GROWTH 2/3 DOWN ONESIDE.
INC- PERIOD	27	DAY 7	60% VEIN GROWTH.
INC- INITIAL PERIOD 25		DAY 9	60% VEIN GROWTH.
WEIGHT	40.40	DAY 11	80% VEIN GROWTH.
LENGTH	5.422	DAY 13	95% VEIN GROWTH.
BREADTH	3.691	DAY 15	COMPLETE VEIN GROWTH.
VOLUME	37.672	DAY 17	LOOKING GOOD.
18% L	0.908827		
13076 L	0.949041		

	DAY 0	DAY 1	DAY 2	DAY 3
WEIGHT	40.40	0.00	39.95	0.00
DENSITY	1.072	1.066	1.060	1.054
DAY LOSS		0.005972	0.005972	0.006636
TEMP	99.5			
WET BULB	80			

DAY 4	DAY 5	DAY 6	DAY 7	DAY 8
39.45	0.00	38.85	0.00	38.30
1.047	1.039	1.031	1.024	1.017
0.006636	0.007963	0.007963	0.007299	0.007299

DAY 9	DAY 10	DAY 11	DAY 12	DAY 13
0.00	37.80	0.00	37.30	0.00
1.010	1.003	0.997	0.990	0.983
0.006636	0.006636	0.006636	0.06636	0.007299

DAY 14	DAY 15	DAY 16	DAY 17	DAY 18
36.75	0.00	36.25	0.00	35.70
0.979	0.969	0.962	0.955	0.948
0.007299	0.006636	0.006636	0.007299	0.007299

DAY 19	DAY 20	DAY 21	DAY 22	DAY 23
0.00	35.20	0.00	34.70	0.00
0.941	0.934	0.928	0.921	0.914
0.006636	0.006636	0.006636	0.006636	0.007299

DAY 24	DAY 25	DAY 26
34.20	0.00	0.00
0.907	ERR	ERR
0.007299	ERR	ERR

Day 24 INITIAL INTERNAL PIP 9.15 AM
Day 25 INTERNAL PIP
DAY 27 PERFECT HATCH
SHELL = 0.20mm
WEIGHT LOSS = 15.3 %

Table 4.1; This is the data I would have on file for any egg that is incubated.

OTHER CONSIDERATIONS

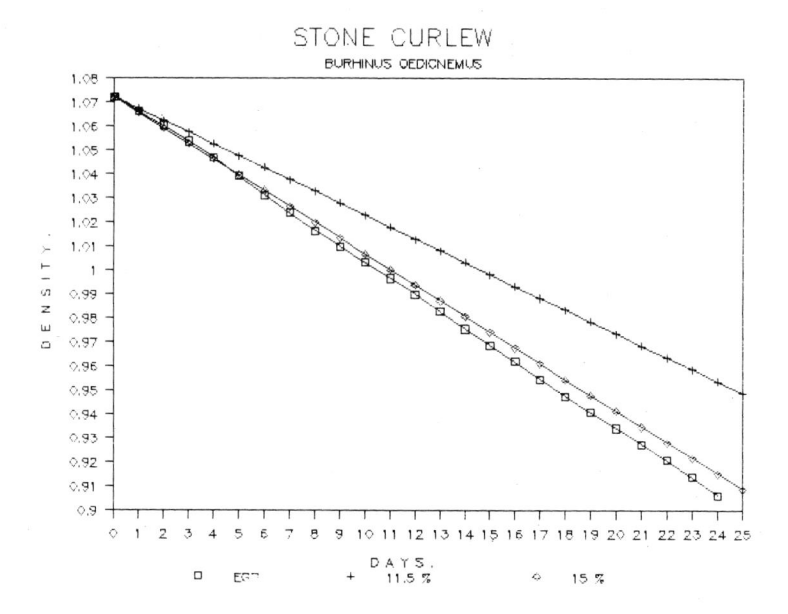

Fig 4.1; This is the type of graph I would have on file for any egg that is incubated.

4.F Computers and monitoring equipment

If you have to incubate large numbers of eggs then a computer can be very useful indeed. It is a good way of keeping records and a program can easily be made up to help with weight loss and density loss techniques.

To give you an idea of the sort of program which can be useful I will show you the one I use.

The following table, 4.2, shows you what I would have on the computer screen for each egg that has to be incubated. This particular one is for a Satyr Tragopan egg.

As you can see information about the egg is filled in on the left hand side. The computer then works out the volume of the egg and the density of the egg.

All I have to do then is to weigh the egg every day or every other day and enter the weight of the egg under the corresponding day. The

OTHER CONSIDERATIONS

	A	B	C	D	E	F	G	H
1	SPECIES	GALLIFORMES	PHASIANIDAE		TRAGOPAN	SATYRA		
2								
3	PEN		SUMMARIES >) >> >> >>)> >>					
4	EGG NO		DAY 0					
5	DATE							
6	INC-P	28						
7	INCAP	26						
8	WEIGHT	0.00						
9	LENGTH	0.000						
10	BREADTH	0.000						
11	VOLUME	0.000						
12	18% - L	ERR						
13	13% -L	ERR						
14		DAY 0	DAY 1	DAY 2	DAY 3	DAY 4	DAY 5	
15	WEIGHT	0.00	0.00	0.00	0.00	0.00	0.00	
16	DENSITY	ERR	ERR	ERR	ERR	ERR	ERR	
17	DAY LOSS		ERR	ERR	ERR	ERR	ERR	
18	TEMP							
20								

Table 4.2; A blank file for a Satyr tragopan egg.

computer will then work out the density of the egg and the density loss.

The computer automatically plots a graph with three lines on it. They are the two weight loss lines of 11.5% and 15% plus the line showing the actual weight loss or density loss for the particular egg.

The top right of the computer screen in the diagram is where any information on candling the egg is stored and if there is any information about the egg when it was picked up eg. was it sat on, did it have any cracks, froin a clutch of X number of eggs etc.

Also as I have found that certain species of bird eggs need turning in different ways for maximum results, it would be a good idea to record how you are turning the egg.

The display moves to the left so the weight of the egg can be entered for any number of days.

This particualar program took only four days to write and has saved me hundreds of hours of work.

Fig.4.2, is what might be seen at day 3 after the three measurements have been entered into the computer (length, breadth and weight of the egg on day 0) and the weight of the egg on day 1,2

OTHER CONSIDERATIONS

and 3. The Y axis can be shown as the weight of the egg or as the density of the egg.

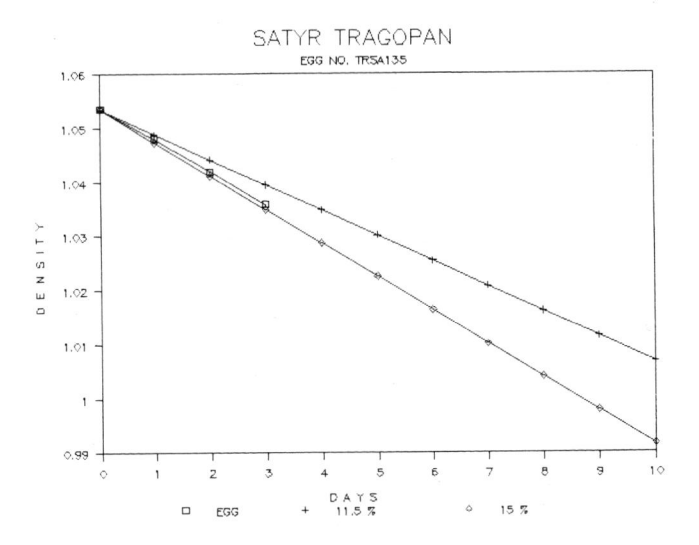

Fig 4.2; What the graph on the computer would show after three days of incubation for a typical Satyr tragopan egg.

Monitoring equipment

It took me six months to find a company who could build a monitoring system for my incubation room. The system was very expensive but it has paid for itself many times over.

Basically there is a probe in each incubator measuring the temperature. The monitoring system is linked directly into the computer.

The system allows me to see exactly how the temperature in an incubator has fluctuated over a set period of time. Via the computer I can set the monitoring equipment to take a reading every minute or every 30 minutes and display the readings on a graph.

OTHER CONSIDERATIONS

Table.4.3.

The following is what is displayed on my computer screen when it is in the monitoring mode.

Probe	Temperature	Low limit	High limit	Warnings
1	36.4	35.0	38.0	
2	24.5	0.0	37.5	*OFF*
3	37.5	36.0	38.3	
4	36.6	35.0	37.5	
5	37.8	36.0	38,3	
6	37.8	36.0	38.3	
7	37.8	36.0	38.3	
8	36.1	35.0	37.8	
9	37.7	36.0	38.3	
10	0.0	0.0	0.0	*OFF*
11	0.0	0.0	0.0	*OFF*
12	0.0	0.0	0.0	*OFF*
13	21.4	15.0	30.0	
14	32.5	29.0	35.0	
15	33.9	30.2	35.2	
16	33.3	29.2	36.0	

Date: 17-04-90 Time: 11:52:22

As you can imagine this is very useful when testing a new incubator out or setting up existing incubators at the start of the incubation season. I also have some probes going into the rearing room in order to monitor the brooders.

An important feature of the monitoring equipment is that it provides an alarm system. For every incubator I can set a high and a low alarm limit. For example if I am running an incubator at 37.5°C then I would set the high alarm at 38.3°C and the low alarm at 36.5°C

During the day the alarm is a bell. At night the computer is linked to a digital communicator which will phone me up if there is a high/low alarm or if there is a power cut. As you can imagine this allows me to be able to go home without worrying if an incubator is going to fail or if a fuse blows.

If I do not answer my phone when an alarm is triggered at night then the digital communicator will try the next phone number which is my sisters house and so on.

PRACTICAL INCUBATION

Within two weeks of installing this system an incubator was accidentally left off at night. After 40 minutes the temperature had dropped enough to set the alarm off and ten penguin eggs were saved from a chilly night.

I would recommend a monitoring system like this to anyone who has to incubate large numbers of eggs. Incidentally the incubators are still monitored when I am using the computer for other purposes.

See page 16 for a typical graph produced by the computer from readings taken in an incubator every three minutes over a 12 hour period.

5 Reference Section

5.A Incubation periods

Albatross
Royal 79
Wandering 70-80

Amazon
Blue-Fronted 26
Cuban 26-28
Green-Cheeked 24
Hispaniolan 25
Lilac-Crowned 26
Puerto Rican 25-27
Red-Lored 25-26
Spectacled (White Fronted) 24
Yellow-Naped 28-29
White-Fronted 24-25

Anhinga . . . . **.25-28**

Avocet
American 22-24
Common 22-24

Bee Eater
Eurasian 24

Bittern
American 28-29
Australian 25

Eurasian 25
Least 19-20
Little 16-17
Sun 27
Yellow 22

Blackbird
Common 12-15
Red-Winged 11-12

Bustard
Great 25-28
Little 20-21

Buzzard
Common 33-38
Honey 30-35
Long-legged 28
Rough-legged 31

Cacique
White-Bellied 28

Capercaillie
Black-Billed 24
Common 24-28

Caracara
Crested 28

Cassowary
Twin-Wattled 49-56

Chaffinch
Eurasian 11-13

Cockatiel 18-20

Cockatoo

Bare-Eyed	23-24
Black	28
Blue-Eyed	30
Citron Crested	25-26
Galah	22-24
Gang-Gang	30
Glossy	29
Goffin's	25
Greater Sulphur	27-28
Leadbeater's	26
Lesser Sulphur	24-25
Medium Sulphur	26-27
Moluccan	28-29
Palm	28-30
Philippine Red-Vented	24
Red-Tailed Black	30
Slender-Billed	23-24
Triton	27-28
Umbrella	28

Condor

Andean	54-58

Conure

Blue-Crowned	23
Blue-Throated	24-26
Brown-Throated	23
Dusky-Headed	23
Green-Cheeked	22-24
Nanday	21-23
Orange-Fronted	30
Patagonian	24-25
Pearly	25
Sun	28
White-Eared	27

Coot

Old World	21-24

Cormorant
Galapagos 23-25
Great 28-29

Crane
Australian 35-36
Black-Necked 31-33
Canadian Sandhill 27
Common (Eurasian) 28-31
Crowned 28-31
Demoiselle 27-30
Florida Sandhill 31-32
Greater Sandhill 31-32
Japanese 30-34
Sarus 28
Siberian White 29
Stanley 29-30
Wattled 35-40
White-Naped 28-32
Whooping 30

Crow
Carrion 18-20

Curassow
Nocturnal 26-30

Curlew
Eurasian 29
Long-Billed 30
Stone 21-23

Dowitcher
Short-Billed 20
Long-Billed 20-21

Duck
African Black 28

REFERENCE SECTION

American Widgeon	26
Australian Grey Teal	26
Australian White-eye	26
Australian Wood (Maned Goose)	30
Baer's Pochard	27
Bahama Pintail	26
Baikal Teal	26
Barrows Golden-Eye	30
Black Scoter	28
Blue-Winged Teal	26
Brazilian Teal	26
Bronze-Winged	30
Canvasback	26
Cape Shoveler	26
Cape Teal	26
Chestnut-Breasted Teal	26
Chilean Pintail	24
Chilean Teal	26
Chiloe Wigeon	26
Chinese Spotbill	28
Cinnamon Teal	26
Comb	30
Common Shoveler	26
Common White-eye	26
Crested	30
Cuban Tree	30
European Eider	27
European Golden eye	28
European Pochard	27
European White-Winged Scoter	28
European Widgeon	26
Eyton's Whistling	30
Falcated Teal	26
Florida	28
Fulvous Whistling	28
Gadwall	26
Garganey	24
Goosander	30

Greater Brazilian Teal	27
Greater Scaup	28
Green-Winged Teal	25
Grey	28
Harlequin Duck	30
Hartlaub's	32
Hawaiian	28
Hooded Merganser	28
Hottentot Teal	25
Indian Spotbill	26
Javan Whistling	28
Kerguelen Pintail	26
King Eider	22
Laysan Teal	28
Lesser Scaup	27
Long Tailed	23
Mallard	28
Mandarin	28
Marbled Teal	26
New Zealand Brown Teal	28
New Zealand Scaup	26
New Zealand Shoveler	26
North American Black	27
North American Ruddy	24
North American Wood	28
Northern Pintail	26
Philippine	26
Puna Teal	26
Radjah Shelduck	30
Red-Billed Pintail	26
Red-Billed Whistling	28
Red-Breasted Merganser	30
Red Crested Pochard	28
Red Head	28
Ringed Teal	24
Ringneck	26
Sharp-Wing	26
Shelduck *(Tadorna)*	30

REFERENCE SECTION

Smew	28
Southern Pochard	26
Spectacled Eider	24
Spotted Whistling	31
Tufted	26
Versicolor Teal	25
Wandering Whistling	30
White-Faced Whistling	28
Yellowbills	27

Dunlin 21-22

Eagle

African Crowned	49
African Fish	44-45
Bald	35
Bateleur	42-43
Black	43-46
Bonelli's	37-40
Booted	36-38
Golden	43-45
Imperial	43
Lesser-Spotted	38-41
Martial	45
Short-Toed	45-47
Spotted	42-44
Steppe	64-66
White-Tailed	34-42

Egret

Cattle	24
Great White	25
Intermediate	21
Little	21-25
Reddish	25-26

Emu 57-62

Falcon
Eleanora's ... 28
Gyr ... 35
Lanner ... 32-35
Prairie ... 31
Peregrine ... 29-32
Red-Footed ... 28
Saker ... 30

Flamingo
Lesser ... 28
Greater ... 30-32

Francolin
Kenyan ... 21-23

Frigatebird
Magnificent ... 40

Frogmouth
Tawny ... 30

Fulmar
Northern ... 55-57

Geese
Abyssinian Blue-Winged ... 31
Andean ... 30
Ashy-Headed ... 30
Atlantic Brant ... 23
Atlantic Canada *(canadensis)* ... 28
Bar-Headed ... 28
Barnacle ... 28
Black Brant ... 23
Cereopsis ... 35
Crackling Canada ... 28
Dusky Canada ... 28
Eastern Greylag ... 28

Egyptian 30
Emperor 25
European White-Fronted 26
Giant Canada *(maxima)* 28
Hawaiian 29
Kelp 32
Lesser White-Fronted 25
Magellan 30
Magpie 30
Moffitt's Canada 28
Orinoco 30
Pied 35
Pink-Footed 28
Red-Breasted 25
Ross's 23
Ruddy-Headed 30
Russian Bean 28
Snow 25
Spur-Winged 32
Swan 28
Taverner's Canada 28
Western Bean 28
Western Greylag 28
Whitefront 26
Vancouver 28

Godwit
Marbled 24
Hudsonian 24
Bar-Tailed 24
Black-Tailed 24

Goshawk
Common 35-38

Grebe
Great Crested 25-29
Little 20-24

Red-Necked 22-25

Greenshank
Common 24-25

Grouse
Black 26-27
Blue 24-25
Hazel 25
Ruffed 24
Sage 25-27
Sharp-Tailed 24-25
Spruce 21
Willow/Red 21-22

Guinea Fowl
Helmeted 24-25
Vulturine 25-26

Gull
Herring 27-31

Harrier
Hen 29-31
Marsh 31-38
Montagu's 27-30
Pallid 29-30

Hawk
Red-Tailed 28-32

Heron
Black-Headed 25
Capped 26-27
Chinese Pond 18-22
Cocoi 24-26
Eastern Reef 25-28

REFERENCE SECTION

Goliath 28
Great Blue 28
Green-Backed 21-25
Grey 25-26
Indian Pond 24
Japanese Night 17-20
Little Blue 21-23
Malagasy Pond 20
Black Crowned Night 21-22
Purple 26
Rufescent Tiger 31-34
Squacco 22-24
Tricolored 21
White-Backed Night 24-26
White-Faced 24-26
Yellow-Crowned Night 21-25

Hoatzin 28

Hobby 28-31

Hoopoe
European 16-19

Hornbill
Red-Billied 30

Ibis
Bald 24-25
Glossy 21
Hadada 26
Japanese Crested 30
Northern Bald 27-28
Oriental 23-25
Sacred 28-29
Scarlet 21-23

Jaçana
American 22-25

Jackdaw 17-18

Jay
Eurasian 16-17
Siberian 18-20

Jungle Fowl
Ceylon 18-20
Ceylon Spur Fowl 22-23
Green 21
Grey 20-21
Red 19-21

Kea 28-29

Kestrel
Common 27-29
Lesser 29

Kingfisher
Eurasian 19-21

Kite
Brahminy 26-27
Black-Winged 25-28
Red 31-32

Kookaburra
Laughing 25

Lapwing
Spur-Winged 22-24
Common 24-26

Kiwi 75-80

REFERENCE SECTION

Loon
Black-Throated 28-29
Common 29-30

Lorikeet
Fairy 25
Goldie's 24
Johnstone's 21-23
Little 22
Masena's 23-26
Meyer's 23-24
Musk 25
Ornate 26-28
Purple-Crowned 22
Red-Flanked 25
Scaly Breasted 23
Stella's 26-27
Swainson's 25-26
Varied 22
Weber's 27

Lory
Black 25-27
Black Capped 24
Blue-Crowned 23
Chattering 26
Collared 30
Dusky 24
Duyvenbode's 24
Ornate 27
Papuan 21
Purple Naped 24-26
Rainbow 25-26
Red (Moluccan) 24
Tahitian 25
Violet Necked 27
Yellow-Backed Chattering 26
Yellow Streaked 24

Lovebird
Black-Cheeked 24
Black-Winged 25
Fischer's 23
Grey-Headed 23
Masked 23
Nyasa 22
Peach-Faced 23
Red-Faced 22

Macaw
Blue & Gold 26
Buffon's 26-27
Caninde 26
Chestnut-Fronted 28
Green-Winged 26
Hyacinth 26-28
Illiger's 26-27
Military 26
Red-Bellied 25
Red-Fronted 26
Red-Shouldered 24
Scarlet 26
Yellow-Collared 26

Magpie
Azure-Winged 20
Black Billed (Common) 17-18

Merlin 28-32

Moorhen
Common 19-22
Purple 22-25

Oriole
Baltimore 12-14
Golden 14-15

REFERENCE SECTION

Osprey 38

Ostrich 40-42

Oystercatcher
European 24-27

Owl
Barn 32-34
Great Horned 35
Hawk 26-30
Little Scops 24-25
Snowy 33-36
Tawny 28-30

Parakeet
Alexandrine 26-27
Barred 18
Budgerigar 18
Canary-Winged 26
Derbyan 26
Quaker 23
Red-Fronted 20
Rose-Ringed 23-24
Long-Tailed 24
Malabar 27
Moustached 25-26
Sierra 28
Yellow-Fronted 20

Parrot
African Grey 28
Amboina King 20
Australian King 20-21
Blue-Bonnet 19
Blue-Headed 24-27
Blue-Winged 18

105

Bourke's	18
Brown-Headed	26
Ceylon Hanging	19
Double-Eyed Fig	18-19
Eclectus	28
Golden-Shouldered	19
Green-Winged King	20
Hawk-Headed	28
Jardine's	25-26
Mallee-Ringneck	20
Meyers	24-25
Orange-Bellied	21
Paradise	21
Pesquet's	26-29
Phillipine Blue-Naped	26
Phillipine Hanging	20
Pileated	24
Princess	20
Red-Rumped	21
Red-Winged	21
Rock	18
Salvadori's Fig	23
Senegal	24-25
South American Red Capped	23
Superb	20
Swift	20
Timneh African Grey	26
Turquoise	20
Vernal Hanging	22
White-Capped	26-28

Parrotlet

Blue-Winged	18
Pacific	17

Patridge

Chukar	23

English 23
Gray 23-25
Hungarian 24
Red-Legged 23-25
Rock 24-26

Peafowl
Congo 26-28
Green 28
Indian 27-28

Pelican
Brown 28-29
White 29-30

Penguin
Adelie 33-38
Emperor 62-64
Humboldt 36-42
King 51-57

Phalarope
Grey 23-24
Red-Necked 20
Wilson's 20-21

Pheasant
Amherst 23
Blood 28
Blue-Eared 26-28
Blyth's Tragopan 28
Brown-Eared 26-27
Bronze-Tailed 22
Bulwer's Wattled 25
Cabot's Tragopan 28
Cheer 26
Common 24-25

Congo Peacock 28
Copper 24-25
Crested-Argus 25
Crested Fireback 24
Crestless Fireback 23-24
Edward's 21-24
Elliot's 25
Germain's Peacock 22
Golden 23
Great Argus 24-25
Grey Peacock 22
Green 24-25
Himalayan Monal 28
Hume's Bar-Tailed 27-28
Imperial 25
Kalij 23-25
Koklass 21-22
Lady Amherst's 22
Malayan Peacock 22
Mikado 26-28
Palawan Peacock 18-19
Peafowl 28
Reeve's 24-25
Rothschild's Peacock 22
Salvadori's 22
Satyr Tragopan 28
Siamese Fireback 24-25
Silver 25
Swinhoe's 25
Temminck's Tragopan 28
Western Tragopan 28
White Eared 24

Pigeon
Rock 17-19
Wood 17

Plover
Black-Banded Sand 24-25

Black-Bellied 23
Blacksmith 26
Crowned 25
Dotterel 21
Golden 30
Greater Sand 23-25
Kentish 24
Killdeer 28
Kittlitz's Sand 23-26
Little Ringed 22
Piping 27-31
Ringed 22
Wattled 30-32

Prairie Chicken
Greater 24-25
Lesser 25-26

Ptarmigan
Rock 21
White-Tailed 22-23

Puffin
Atlantic 40-43

Quail
Barred 22-23
Bearded Tree 28-30
Black-Throated Bobwhite 24
Bobwhite 22
Brown 18
California 22-23
Chinese Painted 16
Crested 23
Douglas 22
Elegant 22
Eurasian 17-20
Gambel's 22

Harlequin 14-18
Japanese 18
Jungle Bush 21
Mearn's 24-25
Mountain 24-25
Painted Bush 21
Rain 18-19
Rock Bush 18
Scaled 22-23
Spot-Winged Wood 26-27
Stubble 18-21

Quetzel 17-18

Raven
Common 20-21

Redshank
Common 23-24

Rhea
Common 36-40

Roadrunner
Greater 17-18

Roller
Eurasian 18-19

Rook 16-20

Rosella
Eastern 21
Green 21
Western 20
Common 21-25

Ruff 27

Sandpiper
- Green 21
- Marsh 21
- Pectoral 21-23
- Purple 20
- Rock 20
- Semipalmated 17
- Solitary 21
- Spoon-Bill 18-20
- Spotted 15
- Terek 21
- Upland 21
- Western 21

Shag
- European 30

Shrike
- Great Gray 15
- Red-Backed 14-16
- Woodchat 16

Snipe
- Common 20

Sparrowhawk
- Common 33-35
- Levant 30-35

Spoonbill
- African 23-24
- European 25

Stilt
- Black-Winged 24-27

Stint
- Temminck's 20

Stork
Asian Open-Billed 24-25
Black 30-35
Hammerhead 30
Marabou 30
White 30

Storm Petrel
Leach's 41-42
Wilson's 39-48

Swan
Bewick's 30
Black 36
Black Necked 36
Coscoroba 35
Mute 37
Trumpeter 33
Whistling 36
Whooper 33

Tern
Artic 20-22
Caspian 20-22
Gull-Billed 22-23
Sandwich 20-24

Thick-Knees
Water 24

Tinamou
Elegant Crested 17-21

Turnstone
Common 21-22

Turkey
Domestic 28

Wild 28

Vulture
Bearded 55-60
Egyptian 42
King 56-58

Whimbrel 27

Woodcock
Eurasian 20-22

Woodpecker
Black 12-14
Great Spotted 16
Northern Three-Toed 14

Yellowleg
Greater 23-25
Lesser 21-23

5.B Manufacturers of incubators

Some of the popular small incubator manufacturers

Kuhl Corp, Kuhl Road, P.O Box 26, Flemington, New Jersey 08822-0026, USA.

The Country Boy Incubator Specialist, 3428 Beret Lane, Wheaton, Maryland 20906, USA.

Brower Incubators, P.O Box 2000, Houghton, Iowa 52631, USA.

Humidaire Incubator Company, 217 West Wayne St, New Madison, Ohio 45346, USA.

Petersime Incubator Co., 300 North Bridge Street, Gettysburg, Ohio 45328, USA.

A.B. Incubators, 1600, 40th Street Ct, Moline, Illinois 61265, USA.

Marsh MFG Inc, 7171 Patterson, Garden Grove, California 92641, USA.

Miller Manufacturing Co Inc, South Saint Paul, Minnesota, USA.

A.B. Incubators Ltd, 40 Old Market Street, Mendlesham, Suffolk. IP14 5SA, England.

Brinsea Products Ltd, Station Road, Sandford, Avon BS19 5RA, England.

Curfew Incubators, Buttons Hill, Southminister Road, Althorne, Essex, CM3 6EN, England.

Patrick Pinker (Game Farms) Ltd, Latteridge, Iron Acton, Briston, BS17 1TY, England.

Grumbach Brutgerate GmbH, Am Breitteil 2, Munchholzhausen, 6330 Wetzlar 13, West Germany.

Werner Schumacher Ing, Landenbach, Oberhessen, West Germany.

5.C Conversion charts

Centigrade/Fahrenheit Conversion table.

°C	°F	°C	°F	°C	°F
20	68	23.4	74.1	26.8	80.2
20.1	68.2	23.5	74.3	26.9	80.4
20.2	68.4	23.6	74.5	27	80.6
20.3	68.5	23.7	74.7	27.1	80.8
20.4	68.7	23.8	74.8	27.2	81
20.5	68.9	23.9	75	27.3	81.1
20.6	69	24	75.2	27.4	81.3
20.7	69.3	24.1	75.4	27.5	81.5
20.8	69.4	24.2	75.6	27.6	81.7
20.9	69.6	24.3	75.7	27.7	81.9
21	68.8	24.4	75.9	27.8	82
21.1	70	24.5	76.1	27.9	82.2
21.2	70.2	24.6	76.3	28	82.4
21.3	70.3	24.7	76.5	28.1	82.6
21.4	70.5	24.8	76.6	28.2	82.8
21.5	70.7	24.9	76.8	28.3	83
21.6	70.9	25	77	28.4	83.1
21.7	71	25.1	77.2	28.5	83.3
21.8	71.2	25.2	77.4	28.6	83.5
21.9	71.4	25.3	77.5	28.7	83.7
22	71.6	25.4	77.7	28.8	83.8
22.1	71.8	25.5	77.9	28.9	84
22.2	72	25.6	78	29	84.2
22.3	72.1	25.7	78.3	29.1	84.4
22.4	72.3	25.8	78.4	29.2	84.6
22.5	72.5	25.9	78.6	29.3	84.7
22.6	72.7	26	78.8	29.4	84.9
22.7	72.9	26.1	79	29.5	85.1
22.8	73	26.2	79.2	29.6	85.3
22.9	73.2	26.3	79.3	29.7	85.5
23	73.4	26.4	79.5	29.8	85.6
23.1	73.6	26.5	79.7	29.9	85.8
23.2	73.8	26.6	79.9	30	86
23.3	73.9	26.7	80	30.1	86.2

PRACTICAL INCUBATION

°C	°F	°C	°F	°C	°F
30.2	86.4	33.8	92.8	37.4	99.3
30.3	86.5	33.9	93	37.5	99.5
30.4	86.7	34	93.2	37.6	99.7
30.5	86.9	34.1	93.4	37.7	99.9
30.6	87	34.2	93.6	37.8	100
30.7	87.3	34.3	93.7	37.9	100.2
30.8	87.4	34.4	93.9	38	100.4
30.9	87.6	34.5	94.1	38.1	100.6
31	87.8	34.6	94.3	38.2	100.8
31.1	88	34.7	94.5	38.3	100.9
31.2	88.2	34.8	94.6	38.4	101.1
31.3	88.3	34.9	94.8	38.5	101.3
31.4	88.5	35	95	38.6	101.5
31.5	88.7	35.1	95.2	38.7	101.7
31.6	88.9	35.2	95.4	38.8	101.8
31.7	89	35.3	95.5	38.9	102
31.8	89.2	35.4	95.7	39	102.2
31.9	89.4	35.5	95.9	39.1	102.4
32	89.6	35.6	96.1	39.2	102.6
32.1	89.8	35.7	96.3	39.3	102.7
32.2	90	35.8	96.4	39.4	102.9
32.2	90.1	35.9	96.6	39.5	103.1
32.4	90.3	36	96.8	39.6	103.3
32.5	90.5	36.1	97	40	103.5
32.6	90.7	36.2	97.2	40.1	103.6
32.7	90.9	36.3	97.3	40.2	103.8
32.8	91	36.4	97.5	40.3	104
32.9	91.2	36.5	97.7	40.4	104.2
33	91.4	36.6	97.9	40.5	104.4
33.1	91.6	36.7	98.1	40.6	104.5
33.2	91.8	36.8	98.2	40.7	104.7
33.3	91.9	36.9	98.4	40.8	104.9
33.4	92.1	37	98.6	40.9	105.1
33.5	92.3	37.1	98.8	41	105.3
33.6	92.5	37.2	99	41.1	105.4
33.7	92.7	37.3	99.1	41.2	105.6

REFERENCE SECTION

Relative Humidity table.

If the dry bulb thermometer is constant, which it hopefully is when incubating eggs, then the wet bulb thermometer reading is directly proportional to the relative humidity.

The following table shows three dry bulb readings at the top. To find the relative humidity in an incubator, find the appoximate dry bulb reading you are using and then the table will show you the relative humidity (RH) is at any given wet bulb temperature (WB)

Dry bulb 36°C		Dry bulb 37°C		Dry bulb 38°C	
WB(°C)	RH(%)	WB(°C)	RH(%)	WB(°C)	RH(%)
19	18	20	19	21	20
19.5	20	20.5	21	21.5	22
20	21	21	23	22	24
20.5	23	21.5	24	22.5	26
21	25	22	26	23	27
21.5	27	22.5	28	23.5	29
22	29	23	30	24	31
22.5	31	23.5	32	24.5	33
23	33	24	34	25	35
23.5	35	24.5	36	25.5	37
24	37	25	38	26	39
24.5	39	25.5	40	26.5	41
25	41	26	42	27	43
25.5	43	26.5	44	27.5	45
26	45	27	46	28	47
26.5	48	27.5	48	28.5	49
27	50	28	51	29	51
27.5	52	28.5	53	29.5	54
28	55	29	55	30	56
28.5	57	29.5	58	30.5	58
29	60	30	60	31	61
29.5	62	30.5	63	31.5	63
30	65	31	65	32	66
30.5	67	31.5	68	32.5	68
31	70	32	70	33	71
31.5	73	32.5	73	33.5	74
32	76	33	76	34	76
32.5	78	33.5	79	34.5	79
33	81	34	82	35	82
33.5	84	34.5	85	35.5	85
34	87	35	87	36	88
34.5	90	35.5	91	36.5	91
35	94	36	94	37	94
35.5	97	36.5	97	37.5	97

5.D Pictures of development in the fowl embryo

Development of the chick embryo in relation to the shell, yolk, albumen and extra-embryonic membranes

by BERYL E. TOLHURST

This series of photographs illustrates the macroscopic development of the domestic fowl. To facilitate identification the number of each plate figure coincides with the number of days of incubation.

The photographs of early development are as follows:

Day 1. The embryo on day 1.
Day 2. The embryo on day 2.
    (a) A general view of the whole egg contents.
    (b) The embryo at approximately stage 7. Note the developing area vasculosa (the ring of blood vessels around the embryo).
Day 3. The embryo on day 3.
    (a) The embryo.
    (b) The embryo *in situ* seen through the air space. Note the primitive blood circulation of the yolk sac.
    (c) The egg contents viewed laterally.
    (d) The egg contents viewed from the broad pole.

From the fourth day the embryo is shown from four or six viewpoints:

    (a) The isolated embryo freed of its extra-embryonic membranes. The orientation of the embryo to the vertical axis is indicated from day 10.
    (b) Days 4 and 5: a view of the embryo within the amnion and with the allantoic sac in place.
    Days 6-9: a view of the embryo *in situ* photographed through the air space, the allantois removed.

Days 10-21: a view of the left side of the isolated embryo.
(c) Days 4-9: a view of the embryo *in situ* with the allantois present.
Days 10-21: a view of the right side of the isolated embryo.
(d) A ventral aspect of the egg contents.
(e) A dorsal aspect of the egg contents.
(f) View of the embryo *in situ,* photographed through the air space.

Days 1,2,3b, also days 4c-9c and days 6b-9b were prepared from fresh, unfixed material. All the other eggs were fixed initially. Different methods had to be employed at different developmental stages. Up to day 9 the embryo was usually fixed in alcohol, this having the advantage of rendering the embryo opaque. From day 10 onwards the eggs could be fixed in formalin, after which the shell was removed. On days 3 (c) and (d) also days 4-9 (d), (e) and (f) eggs were fixed in concentrated hydrochloric acid.

This section and the following photographs are reprinted with the permission of B.E. Tolhurst and Chapman and Hall Ltd. I am very grateful for this service.

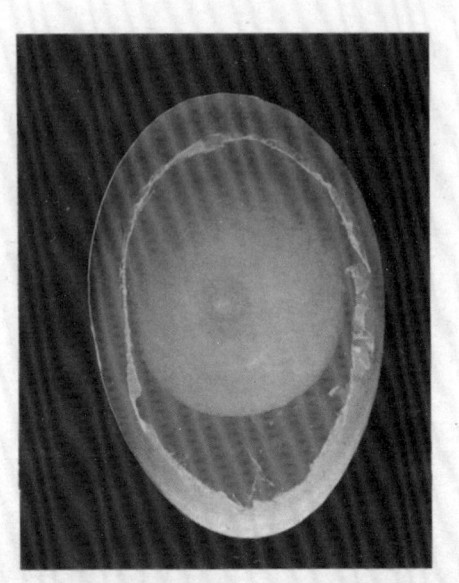

DAY 1

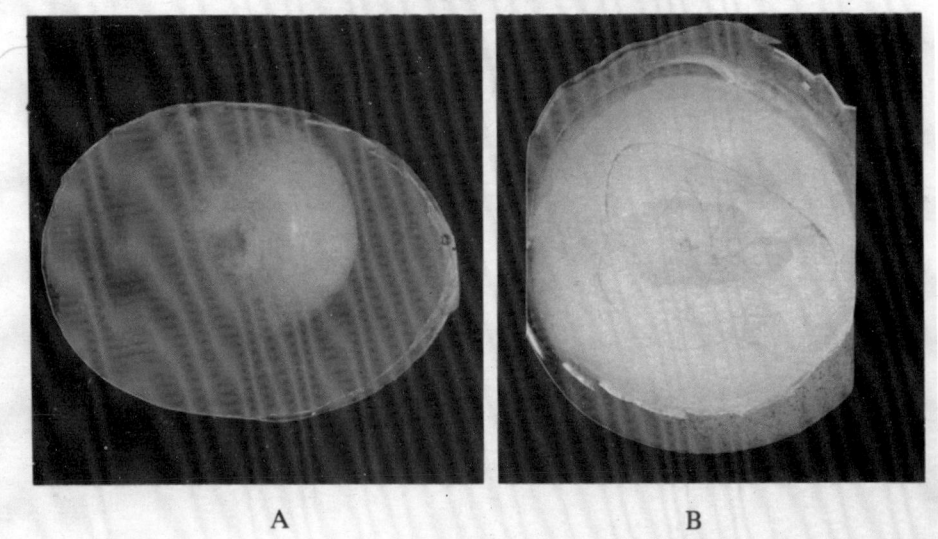

A
B
DAY 2

DAY 3

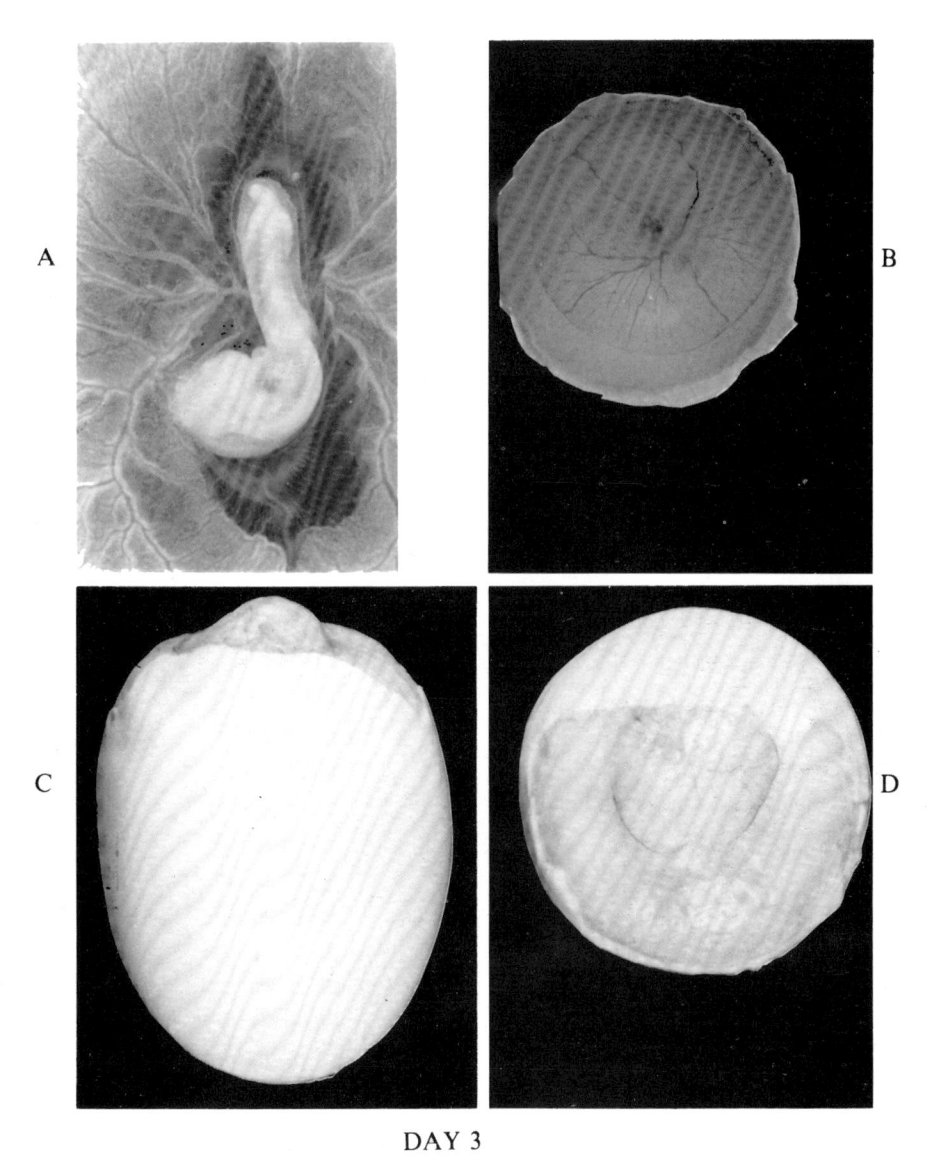

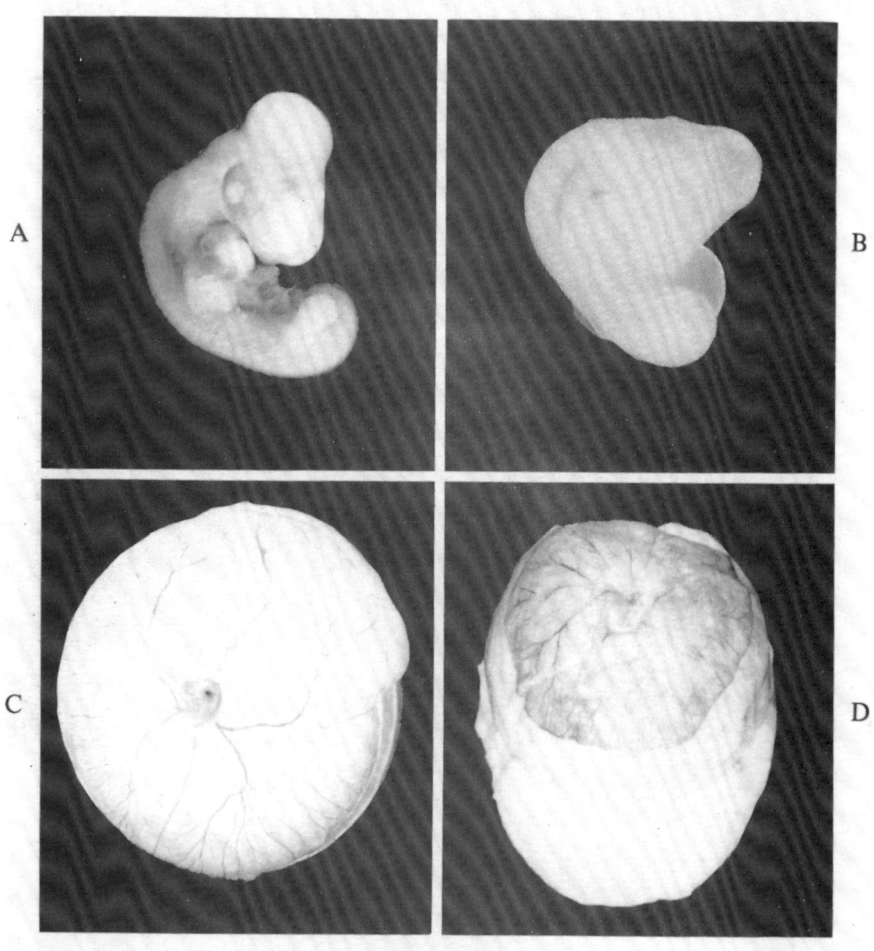

DAY 4

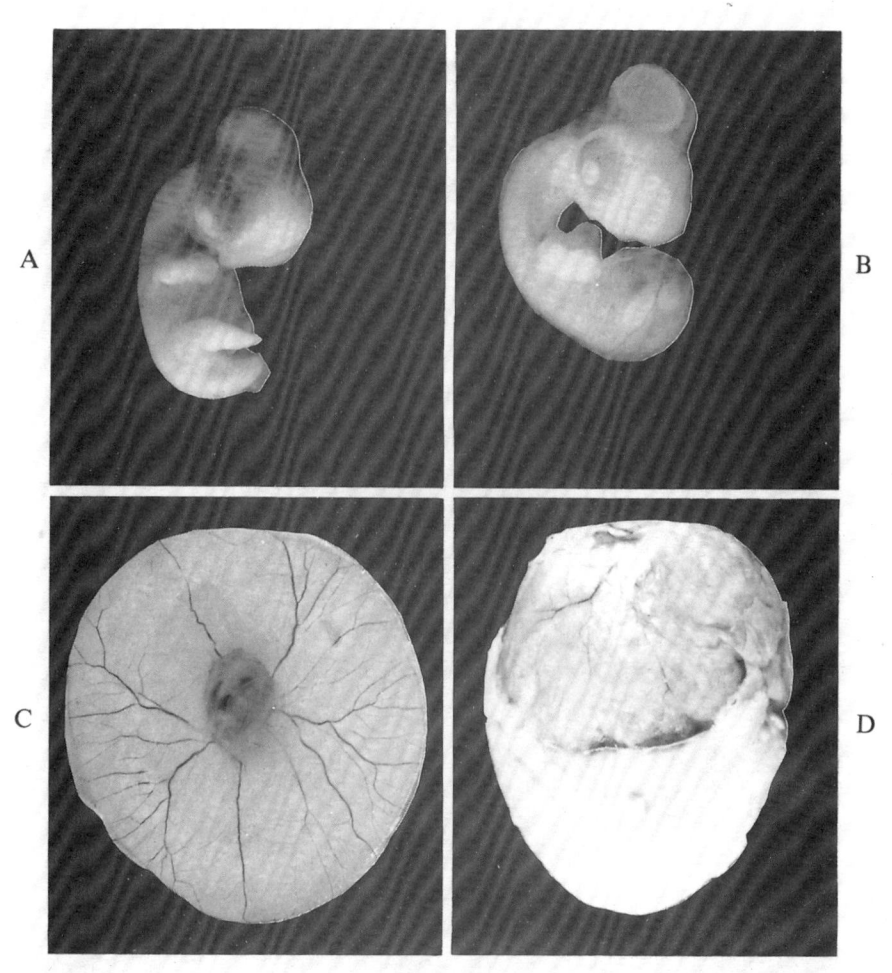

DAY 5

DAY 6

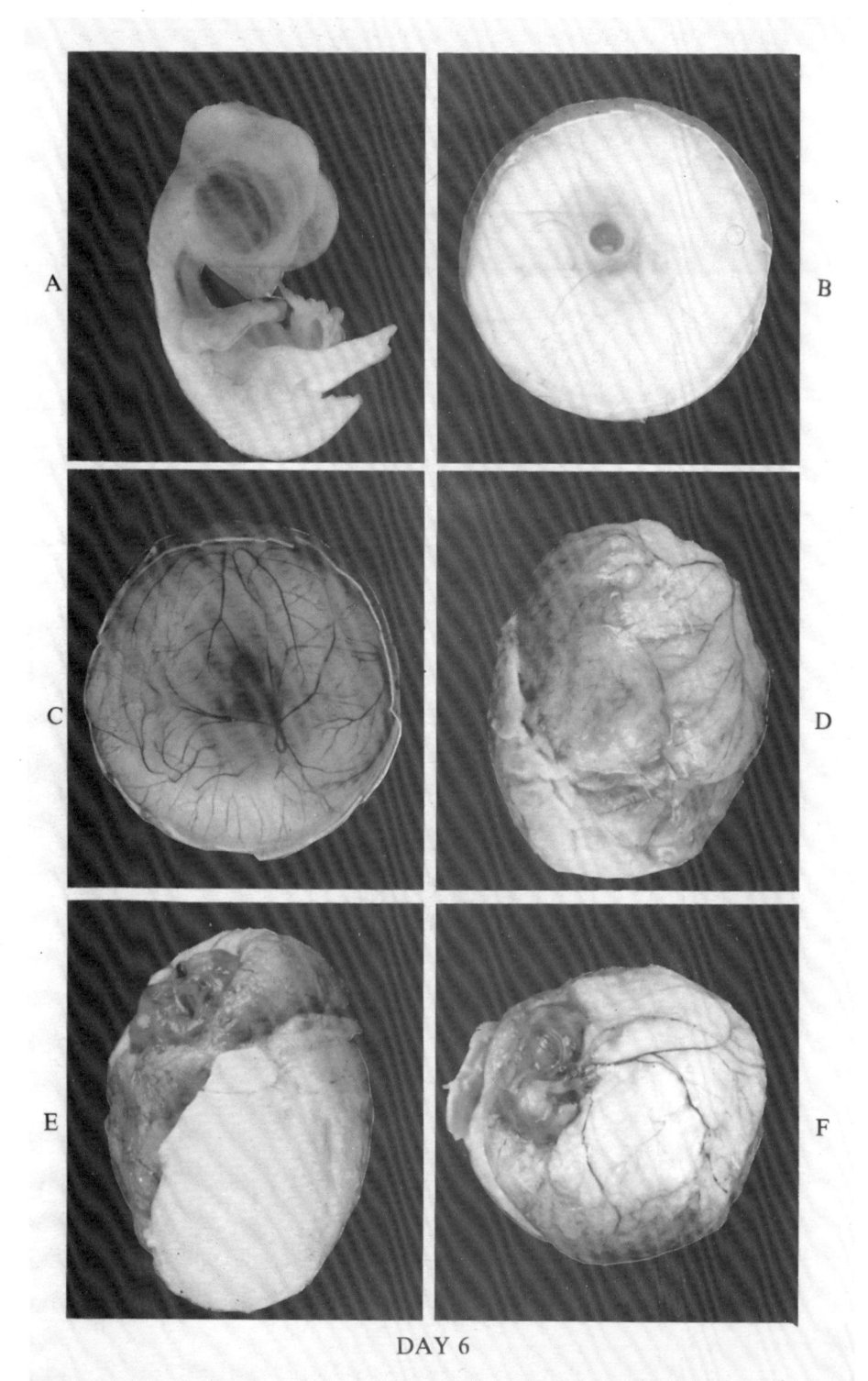

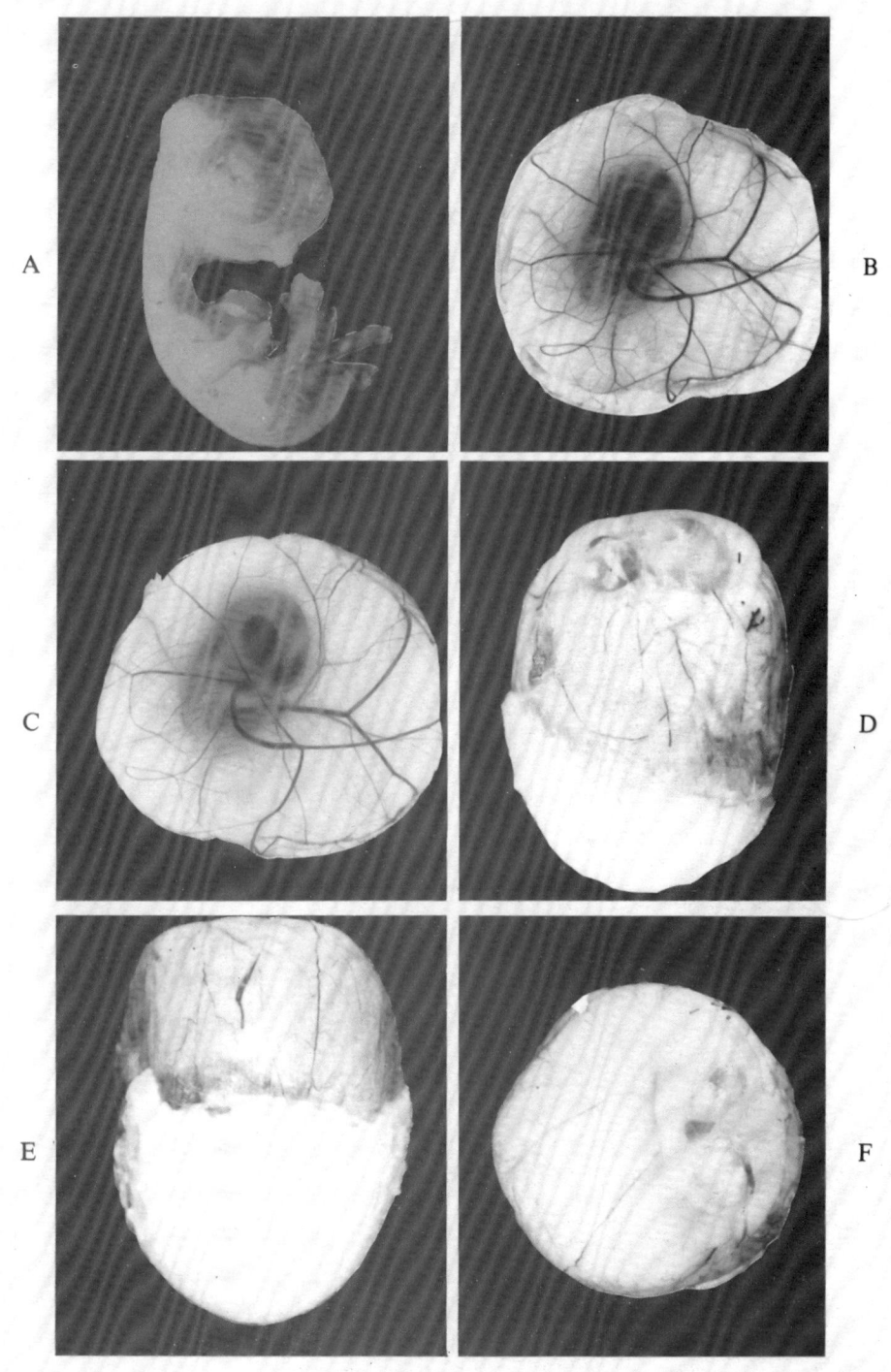

DAY 7

DAY 8

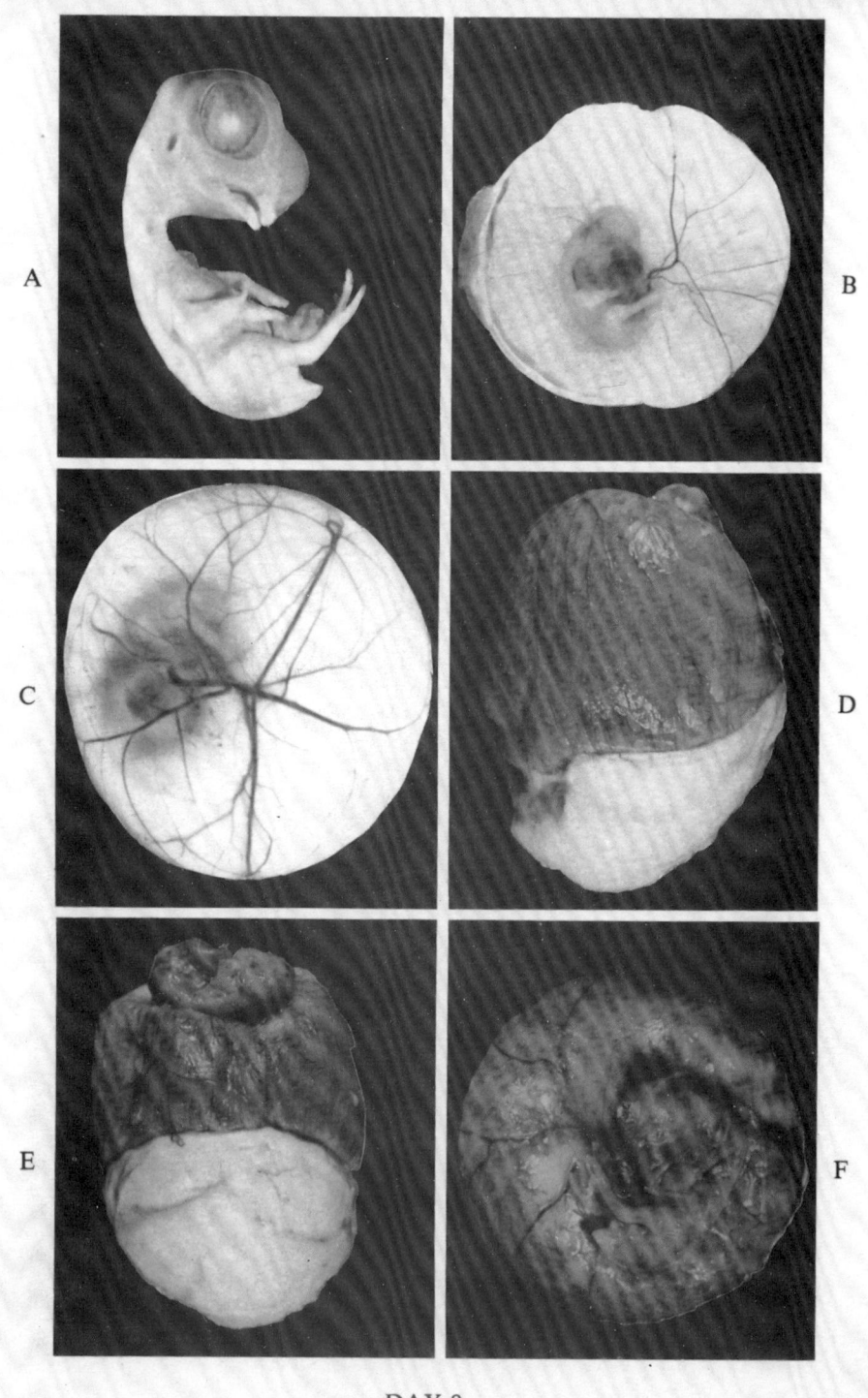

A

B

C

D

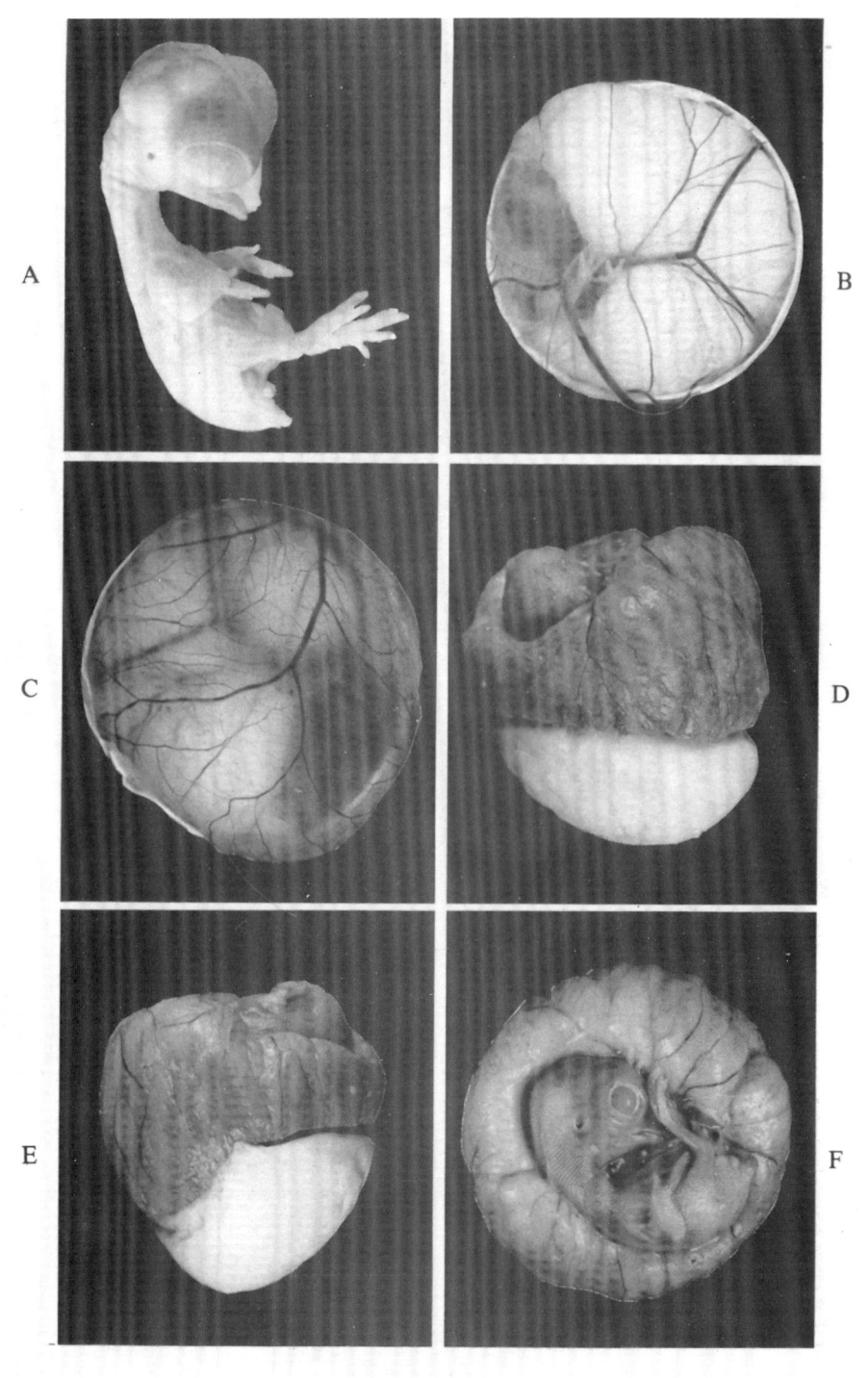

E

F

DAY 9

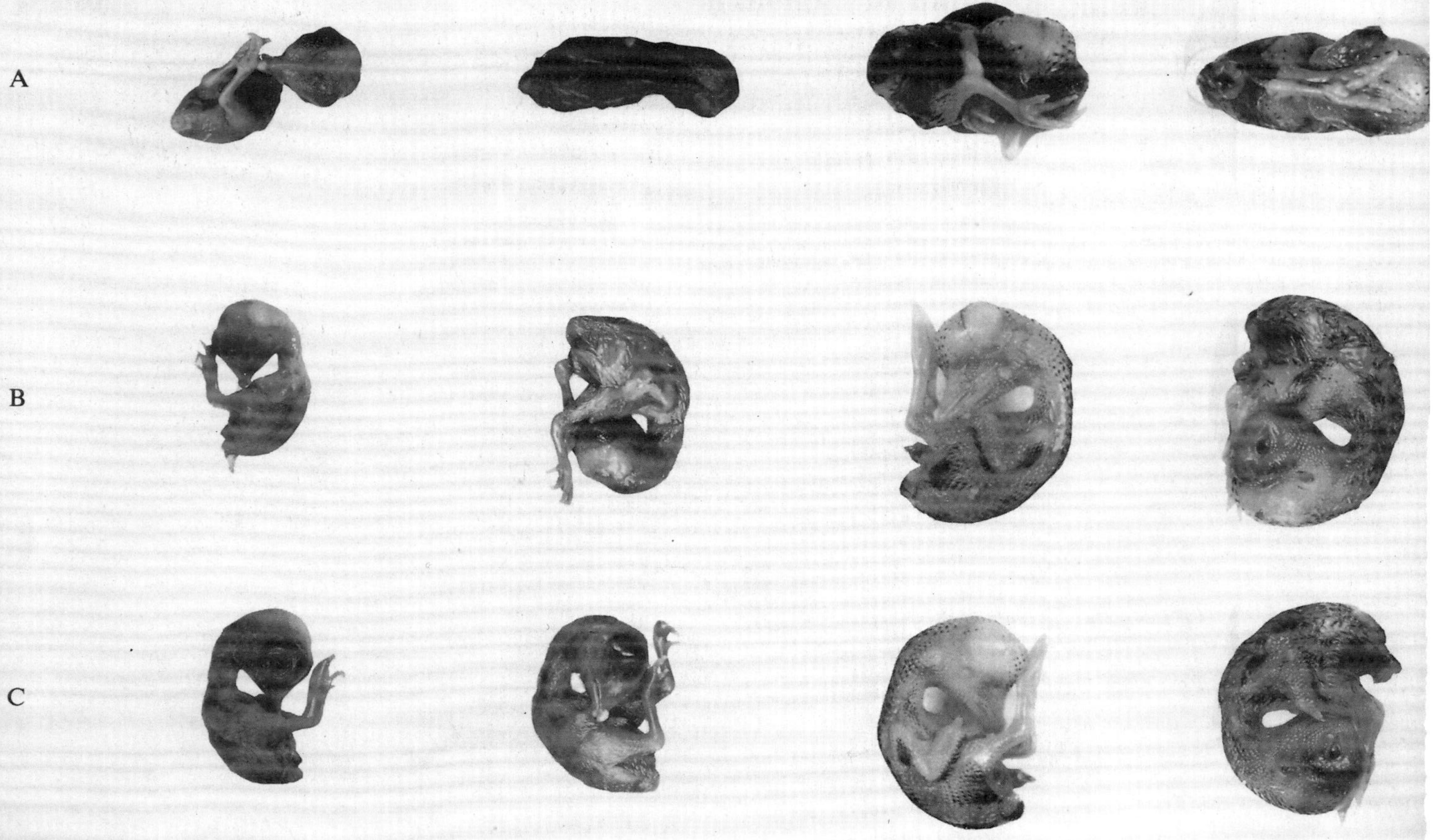
A
B
C

DAY 10 DAY 11 DAY 12 DAY 13

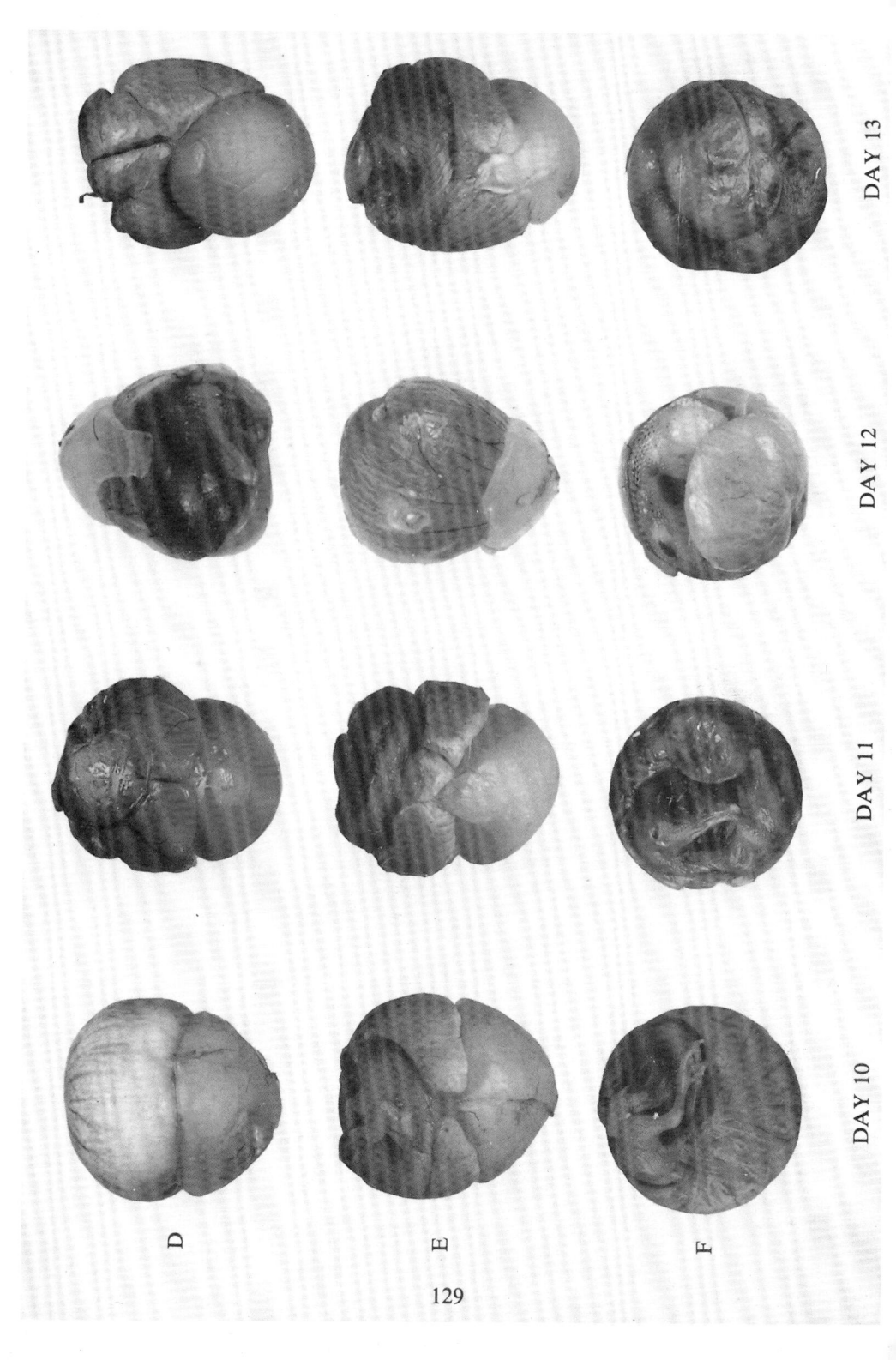

129

A

B

C

130

D

E

F

DAY 14　　DAY 15　　DAY 16　　DAY 17

A

B

C

132

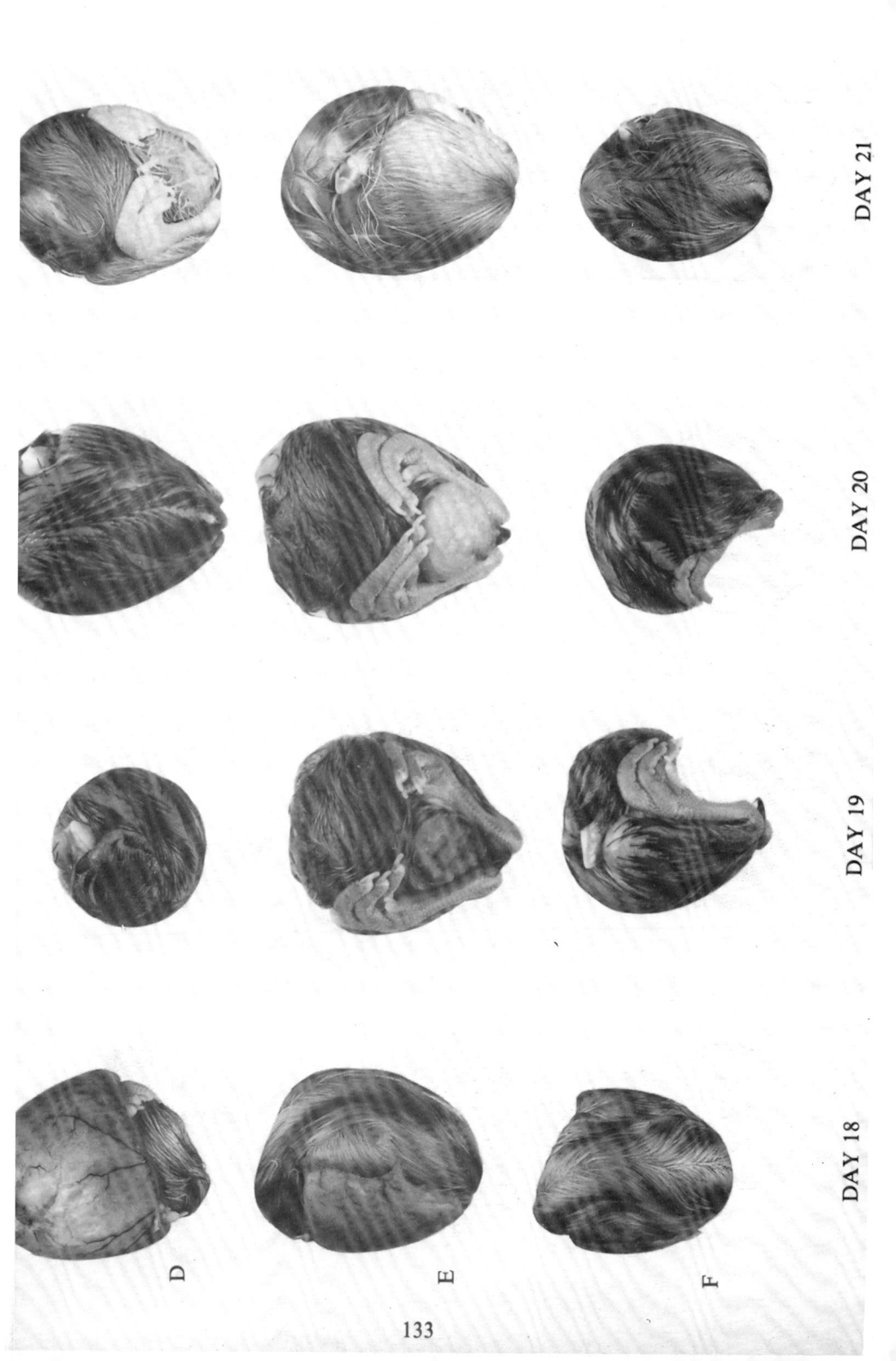

D

E

F

DAY 18   DAY 19   DAY 20   DAY 21

5.E References

Development of the Avian Embryo by B.M. Freeman and Margaret A. Vince. Chapman and Hall.

The Incubation Book by Dr.A.F. Anderson Brown. World Pheasant Association.

Cranes of the World by Paul A. Johnsgard. Croom Helm.

Parrots of the World by J.M. Forshaw. Blandford

The Macdonald Encyclopedia of Birds of the World

Collins Guide to the Birds of Prey of Britain and Europe by Benny Gensbol. Collins.

The Herons Handbook by James Hancock and James Kushlan. Harper and Row.

Wild Waterfowl and its Captive Management by The American Game Bird Breeders Cooperative Federation.

Wading Birds of the World by Eric and Richard Sorthill. Blandford Press.

Parrots Their Care and Breeding by Rosemary Low. Blandford Press.

Index

Bantams 72
Before you start 1
Beware 1
Candling 43
Centigrade/Fahrenheit conversion chart 115-116
Cleaning eggs 18
Clear eggs 81
Computers and monitoring equipment 85
Dead in shell 82
Density loss techniques 55
Detective work on failures 81
Do I incubate or not 3
Early death of embryos 81
Egg collecting 7
Good stock 41
Handling eggs 8
Hatching incubators 39
Hatching time 78
How to clean your incubator 37
Humidity Settings 63
Hygiene 17
Incubation periods 91
Late death of embryos 82
Manufacturers of incubators 114
Monitoring your eggs 43
Monitoring equipment 87
Moving air incubators 24
Nest site hygiene 5
Photos of the daily growth of an embryo 118-133
Problem chart 80
Problems with wet bulbs 22
Records 15
Reference section 91
Relative humidity chart 117
Setting up and testing your incubator 9
Still air incubators 33
Storing eggs 71
The incubation room 8
Thermometers 20
Turning eggs 35
Using broodies and incubators together 77
Weight loss techniques 46
Wet bulb thermometers 21
Which is the best method of incubation for you 4

Robharvey.com Everything for your Bird